CONTEMPORARY QUILTING TECHNIQUES
A Modular Approach

OTHER BOOKS AVAILABLE FROM CHILTON

Robbie Fanning, Series Editor

CONTEMPORARY QUILTING TECHNIQUES

A MODULAR APPROACH

2ND EDITION

PAT CAIRNS

Contemporary Quilting Series

Chilton Book Company
Radnor, Pennsylvania

Published in Radnor, Pennsylvania 19089, by Chilton Book Company

Designed by Anthony Jacobson
Drawings by Carolyn Affleck

On the cover: The Stars at Night. . . . , 33″ × 43″ (82.5cm × 107cm),
Pat Cairns, 1990. Photographer, Jim Conroy; owner, Kathy Wellburn.

Manufactured in the United States of America

Library of Congress/Cataloging-in-Publication Data

Cairns, Pat.
    Contemporary quilting techniques : a modular approach / Pat
Cairns.—2nd ed.
        p.   cm.—(Contemporary quilting series)
        Revised ed. of: Putting it all together. 1st ed. 1987.
        Includes bibliographical references and index.
        ISBN 0-8019-8200-6—ISBN 0-8019-8125-5 (pbk.)
        1. Patchwork   2. Quilting   I. Cairns, Pat.   Putting it all
together.   II. Title.   III. Series.
TT835.C35   1991   91-53042
746.9′7—dc20   CIP

2   3   4   5   6   7   8   9   0   0   9   8   7   6   5   4   3

To
Jean Affleck, 1929–1989,
and
my daughters,
Lynn, Wendy, and Elaine

Contents

Foreword

Some people I know are Anglophiles. They praise any product, person, or experience almost *before* encountering it, as long as it's British.

I'm turning into a Canadianophile, because of authors like Margaret Atwood and Robertson Davies, cities like Vancouver and Toronto, shows like "SCTV" and "Kids in the Hall," and quilters like Jean Affleck and Pat Cairns.

When the first edition of Jean and Pat's book came out in 1987, I was thrilled. At last, somebody had synthesized many of the newer ways of speed-piecing, yet added valuable information to others' techniques. For example, Jean and Pat use Barbara Johannah's revolutionary half-square triangle method—but extend it by bypassing the seam allowance problem of the original method. Before, you would not automatically end up with a square if you didn't use the proper proportions of seam allowance to finished size. Jean and Pat neatly side-step that by using a $\frac{1}{4}''$ seam for the bias seam, planning $\frac{1}{2}''$ seam allowances at the edges, and trimming each square for final accuracy. Brilliant!

Their clear illustrations and friendly tone made me feel as though I'd made new friends while I learned their techniques. But most of all, I was inspired by the color in the quilts. These floating planes of color, misting across the pages, is like quilter's music to me.

Now Chilton and I are pleased to offer a second edition of the book to a wider audience, a book filled with even more Canadian experience than the first edition.

Pat and I hope you, too, are inspired to explore contemporary quiltmaking.

Robbie Fanning
Series Editor

Are you interested in a quarterly newsletter about creative uses of the sewing machine, serger, and knitting machine? For a free sample, write *The Creative Machine*, PO Box 2634, Menlo Park, CA 94026.

Preface

The creation of this second edition of *Contemporary Quilting Techniques* (the first edition was called *Putting It All Together: A Contemporary Approach to Quiltmaking)* is both a happy and a sad occasion for me. To be given recognition by such a well-established figure in the textile arts as Robbie Fanning is a delight, a pinnacle I never dreamt of reaching when the first quilt was made.

But the sadness is with me too. My beloved friend and co-author, Jean Affleck, died of lung cancer in February 1989. We were very different sorts of people, and our friendship grew from our acceptance and enjoyment of the differences and from a basic belief that quilt-making is an art like any other. One masters the technicalities and then makes use of the medium to say what one has to say. Jean believed that life is full of color, surprises, and delights and is always better for another quilt. I agree!

In this new edition, because of the collaborative nature of the original text, there are places where I did not want to change the pronoun "we" to "I," even though I am the sole writer in this case. So please understand that it is not a "royal We," but rather a recognition that the thoughts contained herein are not all mine alone.

I thank Marilyn Banting, Jean Kares, Jean Kuwabara, Paula Pryce, Louise Slobodan, and Birthe Wilson-Achtner for reading and commenting on the text. Their observations were useful and practical. Thanks also to my illustrator, Carolyn Affleck, for her kindness and patience throughout the preparation of the manuscript.

My husband, Alan, deserves special thanks for taking time from a busy schedule to proofread—and for being a great short-order cook!

Pat Cairns
Vancouver, 1991

Preface
to the First Edition

This book began after we had been teaching quilting classes together for several years. We met as members of the Vancouver Guild of Fabric Arts when we were embroiderers, and, discovering we lived near each other on the same street, we became fast friends.

Jean made her first quilt in 1976. She was president of the Vancouver Guild of Fabric Arts when the group sponsored a British Columbia—wide juried quilt show, which she felt she must enter. Pat had started a little earlier, when she and her husband decided they should have a king-sized bed.

Neither of us had a tradition of quilting in our families, and Vancouver, not being yet 100 years old, had very little to show us in the way of examples. So we looked in books, especially those of Jean Ray Laury, and began experimenting. Eventually we discovered the work of Barbara Johannah, and our feelings that quilts need not be made slowly, by hand, on a frame, were reinforced. Our lives have not been the same since. Every quilting book we find we devour; our husbands cannot take us traveling anywhere without frequent stops at fabric stores, and we find quilt ideas and patterns everywhere around us—in nature, in the city, in galleries, and in our own homes. Our object is to share with you the fruits of our search for interesting, reliable ways to make quilts and to encourage you to join us in a lifetime hobby, occupation, or obsession with quilts and quilting, and to find joy in the making.

Pat Cairns and Jean Affleck
Vancouver, 1987

CONTEMPORARY QUILTING TECHNIQUES
A Modular Approach

Introduction

When I make a quilt, I prefer to use methods that do not need a frame. I use the sewing machine whenever possible, because it gives strength to the work, achieves a pleasing result, and seems easier to me. And, of course, the sooner you finish one quilt, the sooner you can start the next.

All of the methods in this book have actually been used by Jean or me to make a whole quilt. We followed each method through to completion, for it often happens that a method seems wonderfully improved on previous methods when used in a sample, but complications appear when making a complete quilt.

While this book does not discuss whole cloth quilts or quilting on a large frame, it does give quite an extensive bibliography, for if ever anything should rival quilts for first place in my heart, it is books! Several of the volumes listed document the traditional processes thoroughly.

In Chapter One I give a list of supplies I use in my own work and describe my work area. In Chapter Two the excitement begins. You will learn how my ideas for a quilt take shape through the use of various design tools. Chapters Three and Four lay out wonderful, new, and quick ways for you to put a quilt together, using The Road to Expo quilt as an example. Of course, there are times when these techniques need to be adapted, and Chapters Five and Six give you some other construction suggestions. The variety of patterns available when you use multistrips is outlined in Chapter Seven. Chapter Eight familiarizes you with making that perennial favorite, the Log Cabin. In Chapter Ten you learn to create beautiful appliqué with your sewing machine. Some less common techniques such as trapunto and puff or bisquit quilts are covered in Chapters Nine and Eleven.

The instructions on how to make the Road to Expo quilt will give you a general working knowledge of our methods. With this knowledge you can make any quilt, in any size you like.

Quilts should be sturdy and appropriate to their use. Wall quilts can be made of delicate fabrics because they are handled very little. If a child of two is to have one of your quilts on his bed, however, the quilt should be able to withstand a lot of loving—and frequent trips to the supermarket!

We enjoy traditional patchwork designs, especially when we can take advantage of the extensive range of fabrics and colors available to the modern quilter. In this way we can reinterpret patterns in a contemporary manner that tells the viewer they were made now, not in grandmother's day. For our quilts we frequently draw an original block. After the fact we often see the relationship with something old.

The whole process of designing is a great learning experience and may reveal to you elements of your environment you would not otherwise notice. Geometric repeats appear in many media and in places you might not have considered, such as diamond bracelets in Sotheby's auction catalog or the Victorian tiled floors of the Royal Museum of Scotland in Edinburgh. They also appear in such everyday places as your gameboards and your kitchen floor. The regularity and flow of geometric designs seem to satisfy some need for order in the human soul.

With the help of this book we would like you to be able to produce quilts that are beautiful, well-crafted, and strong and that have your personal stamp on them. They should also be fairly quick and easy to produce. The construction methods contained in this book are very adaptable. With a little study, you should be able to decide which method is best for your particular design. Almost any design can be adapted to one of the methods we discuss. To paraphrase a local artist, art is problem solving. Find out what you want to do, and then find out how to do it! We hope we can help you solve the problems that you set for yourself.

PART I
BEGINNING

CHAPTER ONE

Supplies and Work Station

SEWING MACHINE

We have heard quilters actually apologize for using their machines—"Yes, I do some quilting, but it's only machine." Goodness! That remark should have gone out with, "I'm only a housewife." Of course you use your sewing machine, and as much as possible. Design for it, and let it help you make as many beautiful quilts as you can.

Machine piece, then hand quilt, or, if you like the effects attainable, machine quilt too. If the work is of high quality, one cannot possibly say that a machine-stitched quilt is inferior to a hand-stitched one. It is like comparing apples and oranges. Don't try to imitate handwork, but, rather, use the machine to make something unique and beautiful in its own right.

Any sewing machine that is in good working order and is properly adjusted to give a well-balanced stitch can be used for quilting. If you and your sewing machine are not getting on well together, go to a reliable dealer and have it serviced. Many times a simple adjustment will improve its efficiency and your disposition enormously. If you are contemplating buying a new sewing machine, here are some special features to look for.

Zigzag stitch. For doing satin stitch and machine appliqué.

De-centering needle. Be sure the machine allows you to move the needle position to the left and right of the center point. You will need this feature when you are working with very narrow strips, as in Seminole patchwork, and want a narrow seam allowance.

Single-hole needle plate. Most machines today have a wide-hole needle plate to accommodate zigzag stitching. But if you are planning to make a quilt by machine and will use straight stitching throughout, a single-hole needle plate will give you better control and less puckering. Or you can use a wide-hole needle plate and de-center the needle. Remember that if you de-center the needle when piecing, it will change the width of your seam allowance if you are matching cut edges rather than following a drawn sewing line. See your sewing machine dealer or the Suppliers list for companies that sell single-hole needle plates.

Flat bed. This is another feature that generally gives you more control over your sewing. I have recently become the proud owner of a used industrial sewing machine, and one of the things I like best about it is the flat bed. No more balancing a big piece of work on a tiny attachment on my portable machine that pretends to be a flat bed! Of course, portable machines have a great many uses, and I'm not suggesting you throw yours away—it's just something to consider in the overall picture if you are buying a machine.

Open-toed appliqué foot. This foot (Figure 1-1) gives you a clear field of vision so that you can see exactly where the next stitch should go when you are appliquéing. A clear plastic foot can also be used for this purpose.

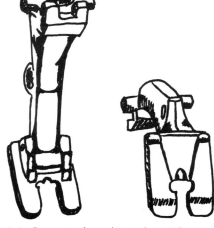

1-1. Open-toed appliqué foot. The underside (right) shows grooves to accommodate satin stitch.

Walking foot or even-feed foot. This attachment (Figure 1-2) provides another set of feed dogs (or some alternative) on top of the fabric. The cloth is thus caught both top and bottom, and the two layers are moved along at the same pace. It is also helpful for matching stripes or plaids and for sewing velvets.

Sewing machine needles. Buy the best quality you can and change them often. Burrs and blunt needles can snag your fabric. Sizes 10(70) and 12(80) are good for general use. Use 14(90) for machine quilting.

SCISSORS

It is best to have several pairs. The most important ones, and the pair to be guarded with your life, are good **shears** for cutting your fabrics. Don't cut anything else with them! Get a cheap pair of scissors for cutting paper and anything containing polyester. A small, sharp-pointed pair of **embroidery scissors** is useful for snipping seams or ripping stitches. I almost always wear a pair on a ribbon around my neck when I am working. That way I know where they are.

Another recent acquisition of mine is a pair of **appliqué scissors** (Figure 1-3). The large, flat blade on the underside allows you to cut very close to the line of stitching without having to worry about cutting the fabric. While these are rather specialized, it is a joy to have good tools if you really like to do machine appliqué.

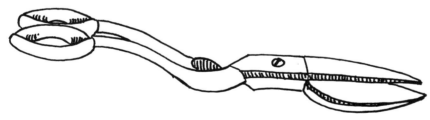

1-3. Appliqué scissors.

Silks, satins, and other easily frayable fabrics are best cut with **pinking shears**.

ROTARY CUTTER AND MAT

These tools are best and most efficient for simplifying and speeding up the cutting of your quilt top. Using the sharp-bladed rotary cutter (Figure 1-4), you can cut straight lines or curves through many layers of fabric quickly and accurately. This cutter must be used with a special self-healing plastic mat to prevent the blade being dulled (and your tabletop ruined). You cannot use a dressmaker's cutting board with the rotary cutter.

A metal or heavy plastic ruler is also needed along with the rotary cutter and self-healing mat for cutting strips and straight lines.

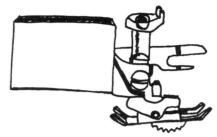

1-2. Even-feed foot.

1-4. Rotary cutter. The large-bladed cutter is the most useful.

DRESSMAKER'S CUTTING BOARD

Cutting boards are readily available wherever sewing supplies are sold. Get the kind that is marked with lines, not dots, and has some diagonal lines included in its markings. These boards are made of corrugated cardboard, and pins can be stuck into them when you want to position fabric accurately. You can spread the board out almost anywhere—on a bed or on a table to enlarge your working surface. I have a work-table surface covered with a cutting board I trimmed to fit and taped in place. This provides a grid constantly ready for use, whether I am making a single square or a huge number of strips.

The dressmaker's cutting board can also be used with a yard/meter stick to cut strips. This system, however, has really been superseded by the self-healing mat and rotary cutter. But it is still useful if you want to try out the strip piecing techniques before investing in the tools necessary for the newer method.

RULERS

An assortment of sizes is useful to have on hand. A **yard/meter stick** of metal with clear markings is the best tool to use if you plan to cut and mark strips on the dressmaker's cutting board.

A **heavy plastic see-through ruler** with lengthwise and crosswise markings on it, about 18–24" (45–60cm) long, and 3–6" (7.5–15cm) wide is most useful. Consider this purchase carefully because you will use it a lot in conjunction with the rotary cutter to cut strips and trim seams.

A **flexible stainless steel ruler with a cork backing** will stay exactly where you put it without pressure and is helpful for people who have arthritis. Canada is in the midst of converting to the metric system; dress pattern and fabric companies have already changed over. It will be difficult for those of us who have grown up with feet and inches, but eventually we will become accustomed to the much simpler metric system. For the moment I still use the old Imperial system (I've put metric measurements in parentheses in this book) because cutting boards and good plastic rulers are not yet generally available with metric markings, at least here in Canada. When metric tools arrive, we can all convert completely. To make life easier for yourself, just remain consistent and use one system of measurement throughout a project. (When revising this book I remade some of the samples, using the metric system, just to make sure the measurements I used in the directions were correct. For more on the metric system, see "Special Note on Seam Allowances" in Chapter 3.)

MARKING DEVICES

The quilt surface should not be marred by any drawn lines. If you are putting any marks on the top of your quilt, test the marker *first* for removability. Some of the new "vanishing" pen marks can later reappear for good. In fact, there seems to be evidence that the fabric begins to deteriorate where these pens have been used. Because I want to make beautiful, long lasting quilts, I don't use these pens. Also, I never iron any marking after I put it on a quilt top, nor do I leave it lying around in the sunlight. Heat and light are great chemical reactors.

To test a marking device. Take a scrap of the quilt top fabric, mark it, and submit it to whatever treatment, such as washing, ironing, or dry-cleaning, you think the quilt may ever get. If there are no marks left on the fabric, then you can use that form of marking on that fabric. Here are some suggestions for marking devices:

Soft drawing pencils (2B through 6B). These are best for marking lines on the underside of the fabric. Very little pressure is needed to make a mark because the leads are so soft. Keep them sharp so that the lines are accurate. A friend has suggested to me that a mechanical pencil is excellent for this purpose. The leads are always sharp, and the line is fine.

Colored pencils. The leads in these pencils, used by both artists and schoolchildren, are of a chalky consistency, and there are many colors available. Use them to mark stitching lines on the wrong side of the fabric and to mark hand quilting lines on top of the fabric. Use a *dotted* line for marking the quilt top, in a color as close to that of the quilting thread as you can get. The marks will usually all have disappeared by the time you have finished quilting. Brands to look for are Prismacolor, Derwent, and Faber-Castell.

Watercolor pencils. These pencils can be either graphite or colored and are meant to disappear when washed with water. Still, they should be tested on your cloth before use. Prismacolor also manufactures these pencils.

Soap. Old, hardened slivers of soap make great markers for dark fabrics and completely disappear with steam.

Masking tape. This inexpensive tape comes in various widths. It can be a useful marking device when your quilting pattern is made up of straight lines. Apply it to your work and quilt along one or both sides. The same piece of tape can be used several times. Keep your work out of sunlight when it has masking tape on it. And tape just what you will be able to quilt in one sitting because it can be difficult to remove after being left on the cloth for any length of time and leaves a residue.

Removable transparent tape. This tape can be used on satins and other delicate fabrics without leaving marks. The same precautions should be observed as those noted above for masking tape.

Dressmaker's carbon paper. This is useful when you wish to transfer a complex quilting pattern to your cloth. Select a carbon paper as close in color to your quilting thread as possible, and transfer the pattern with a *dotted* line. Test it first on a scrap of fabric.

STRAIGHT PINS

The best ones are extra long, about $1\frac{7}{8}$" (5cm) glass-headed pins. They don't get lost in the batting, are easy to insert and remove, and go through the three layers of the quilt with ease.

SAFETY PINS

Get pins of good quality, about $1\frac{1}{2}$" (4cm) long (Figure 1-5). They are useful when you are pinning the three layers together in preparation for machine quilting. They are used *between* the quilting lines, which will still require pinning with the more easily removed glass-headed pins.

PAPER

Many kinds of paper can be helpful in your design work. You will find, after a bit of experimenting, that some methods of using papers are more congenial to you than others, and that not all of the following will be necessary.

Graph paper. This paper comes in sheets, pads, rolls, and notebooks. It provides a ready-made grid for drawing geometric patterns, tracing small designs for later enlargement, sketching, and mapping out cutting diagrams. Nonreproducible grids are available for photocopying your designs so that the grid does not show.

Tracing paper or layout paper. Available in sheets, pads, or rolls, it is translucent and can be placed over any design for tracing. It can be used to try out various quick color renditions or to alter designs so that they do not have to be redrawn.

Heavy drawing paper, oak tag, or thin cardboard. Any of these heavier papers comes in handy when a full-size drawing (called a cartoon) of your block is required, or for templates when only a few patches are needed. Cardboard cereal boxes are good for this work, too—and economical.

SHEET PLASTIC

This is the preferred material for making templates. It is very firm, easily cut with scissors, and thick enough to draw around. Used X-ray films are the right thickness also.

These transparent materials allow you to place your template so that you can take advantage of the patterns on your fabric. The best sheet plastics are marked with a grid and have a slightly roughened surface to prevent slipping when you draw around the template.

CALCULATOR

A simple one will come in handy for figuring yardages.

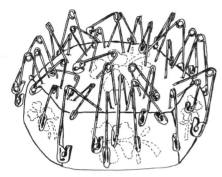

1-5. Open safety pins in a pin cushion. This is the best way to keep them; otherwise you are always fastening, unfastening, or untangling them.

IDEA FILE

This is one of your most important tools. Pick up some sort of notebook, sketch book, or three-ring binder into which you can put your own doodles and sketches, designs and color arrangements, clippings from magazines, or photographs you have taken of interesting forms and designs. Don't limit yourself to quilt themes and images when seeking ideas. Anything you enjoy visually may come in handy someday in your work as a quilt designer.

You will find that these books you create become a sort of visual diary of your response to the world around you and of the progress you are making in being able to express your ideas. Mine are very precious to me and are the first things I would rescue in an earthquake!

IRON

A good steam iron is a necessity (Figure 1-6). Pressing is one of the most important influences on the final product in piecing or appliqué. The new models even turn themselves off if you forget to do so.

LINT ROLLER

This is a wonderful device for keeping threads and lint off the surface of your quilt.

HAND-QUILTING NOTIONS

Needles. Quilting needles are very short and are sometimes called "betweens." A size 7 or smaller (the smaller the size, the larger the number) will produce a nice stitch.

Thimble. Some people can use one; others cannot. Try one on your pushing finger and persevere a bit to see if you can learn to use it. If you find you can't, forget it. Jean Ray Laury doesn't use one, and look where she is! Some people, in fact, use two thimbles—one on each hand, on top and below the quilting surface.

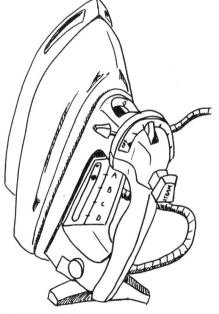

1-6. Steam iron.

QUILT BATTING

The bonded or glazed polyester batting available today is far superior to the cotton or wool used in former times. It withstands washing without bunching or lumping and retains the high loft with which the quilt began. It is available by the yard (meter) or in prepackaged, bed-sized pieces. The thickness of the batt varies from very thin and supple for hand quilting to a thicker, tougher batt for machine quilting. There are also very thick batts to be used for tied comforters.

There is, however, a possible disadvantage to the use of polyester batting, and that is the phenomenon called **bearding**. Bearding refers to the batting that works its way through the spaces between the threads of the encasing layers of fabric to produce little pills on the surface of the quilt. It is most noticeable on dark fabrics. The ideal solution to this problem has not been found, but following is some information on how to keep bearding to a minimum.

Thread count of the quilt fabric. The closer the weave (the more threads per inch/centimeter), the less likely that the polyester batt will work its way through to the surface.

Fiber content of the quilt fabric. Cotton seems better than polyester for preventing bearding. Man-made fibers are very smooth, and perhaps this smoothness allows the batt fibers to slip through more easily than they do through cotton fibers.

Weight of the quilt fabric. A heavier weight of fabric seems to offer more resistance to the batting fibers. If you must use a thin, loosely woven fabric because the color is wonderful, it can be lined with white cotton. Again, the closer the weave, the better the barrier to bearding.

Fiber content of the batting. Cotton won't beard, but must be quilted closely. Its fibers are short and will shift into lumps unless firmly anchored into place with quilting stitches. It has less loft than polyester batting. There are new cotton/polyester batts that have been formulated to overcome the problems of each kind of batt by combining the fibers into one. They must be carefully washed before use. This is certainly an area of quilting in which new technology may produce valuable products.

Bearding is, under normal circumstances, more pronounced on the back of the quilt because of the friction caused by rubbing against a blanket or sheet. Therefore take special care in choosing the backing fabric, keeping in mind the above factors.

THREAD

Use good quality thread. Your stitches are meant to stay there a long time. They are under stress when the quilt is lifted and moved about, especially when it is being washed and is heavy with water. At times I have used cotton-wrapped polyester thread, 100% polyester thread, and 100% cotton thread. A good quality 100% cotton thread is a joy to use for hand quilting.

One thing I don't use is transparent nylon thread. I find it stretchy and difficult to work with. I don't like the idea of pretending that the stitching and its color aren't important and therefore can be discounted when designing. Some methods of machine quilting earnestly try to create quilts that look "just like handwork," which seems to me false and imitative. In the nineteenth century when the sewing machine was introduced, it was taken up enthusiastically for piecing. Now it is time for us to go a step further and create new contemporary machine sewing styles.

FABRIC

As a potter needs to understand her clay, so a quilter needs to understand her fabric. What are its qualities? What can you expect it to do, or not do? The best to work with is 100% cotton fabric of good quality in a dress weight. It has a little bit of stretch, just enough to allow for the correction of a tiny error here and there. Cotton will hold a press put there by your fingers, or by an iron, and many times it does not need pins to keep it in place when you are stitching.

The ideal cloth should be firmly woven. It should also be opaque, so that seam allowances won't show through. Seldom is this ideal cloth found, however, and generally color is the main criterion for the inclusion of a fabric in a design.

Much of the cloth available comes in broadcloth weave, which has more warp threads (lengthwise) than weft threads (from selvage to selvage). Because of the weave, the color of a solid-color broadcloth may change if it is cut and used with the weft going in different directions in different pieces. (This seems to be most noticeable in the shiny, thin polyester/cotton blends.) Just keep this phenomenon in mind if your design would be disrupted by this kind of color change. Most often it is a very regular repeat pattern that is affected. If necessary, these fabrics can be treated like a napped cloth and the top of each piece marked in some way.

The thin polyester/cotton blends of broadcloth weave have other drawbacks too. Although they are readily available, inexpensive, come in a wonderful color range, and wear forever, I do not recommend them for quiltmaking. Often they are so thin that the seam allowances become prominent and detract from your overall design. They do not keep their press, they do not tear cleanly, and they fray readily. But worst of all, when they are used with polyester batting, there is a greater likelihood of bearding. If I do use thin polyester/cotton blends, I line them with thin white cotton, each piece separately. It is well to line silks and other slippery fabrics also. It is then much easier to handle them. Simply cut and mark the lining fabric as though it were the real thing. Cut the silk or slippery fabric and pin the two together, with the pins in the seam allowance. Then proceed as though they were a single piece of fabric and join them to the other pieces in your design. By doing so you will find these difficult fabrics much easier to handle, and you will probably save time in the long run.

Fabrics are right up there with quilts and books as one of my addictions. I practice what my friend Frances Fournier calls "creative overbuying." That is, when I see a fabric I really like, whether or not I need it right now, I buy some. Fashion dictates the range of colors available each year, and unless you build a collection of fabrics, you may not find the color you need in a store. If you have no specific end product in mind when you buy, it is difficult to answer the question "How much?" If the fabric is a print, two or three yards (meters) will usually allow its useful inclusion in some future projects. Solid colors are often more difficult to come by and should be added to your palette of fabrics in as large amounts as you can afford. And, of course, the fashion in quilts just now is to use many more fabrics than a few years ago—so you don't need as much of each one.

Many people think only of tiny flowered prints when they think of quilts. This may be a safe choice, but not necessarily very interesting, especially if more than one print is contained in the design. Try to select a variety of scales and types of prints (Figure 1-7). Dots, flowers, stripes, and paisleys can be combined happily to give exciting designs. Be aware that the same print can look very different when viewed close up and when seen from across the room. Step back several feet to get a perspective before making your final selection.

When you find yourself face to face with a wonderful piece of fabric in a store, and a half-formulated idea for a quilt in your mind, ask yourself these questions:

1. Is the fabric to be used in the border? Is it reasonable to buy the amount of fabric required for a border that is all in one piece? If so, can the rest of the width of the fabric be used elsewhere?

2. What is the area, roughly, of the pieced top? How much of it will be made with the fabric being considered?

3. How big are the pieces, with how many seams, and how big are the seam allowances? For instance, a patch that is 2" (5cm) square finished, when $\frac{1}{2}$" (1cm) seam allowances are added, increases in area from 4 square inches (25 square cm) to 9 square inches (49 square cm), which is a lot. But an 8" (20cm) finished square increases from 64 square inches (400 square cm) to only 81 square inches (484 square cm) when $\frac{1}{2}$" (1cm) seam allowances are added, which is not nearly so great an increase. Can you estimate whether the addition of the seam allowances increases the fabric requirements by an equal amount, by half, by a quarter?

4. How much extra should be added to make up for shrinkage?

5. Does the fabric have an "up and down," or nap, that needs to be considered?

6. Have you left room for error, flaws, and other unexpected events? When you make your calculations roughly and quickly like this, always err on the side of "roominess." Give yourself a bit extra to play with. I can guarantee that the fabric won't be there in a few weeks when you need "just another quarter yard (meter)" to finish an elegant design.

7. Is the fabric being used as a backing? Backing fabrics can be tricky and may require more fabric than one would first estimate. If the quilt module measures more than one half the width of the fabric, allow a full width for each piece of the backing required. You can always use the extra backing fabric in the pieced top.

1-7. Patterned fabrics. A variety of scales and patterns pleases the eye.

BACKING FABRIC

A firmly woven 100% cotton is the fabric of choice. For machine quilting it is decidedly the best. Blends and other slippery fabrics tend to create a lot of troublesome puckers in the undersurface, whereas a good-weight cotton fabric seldom does.

Flannelette or brushed cotton can be a good selection for a child's quilt. It prevents the quilt from sliding and is warm and comforting.

Make the backing fabric part of your overall design. It may be a fabric you have already used in the top. It may be plain or figured. Stripes or prints with a strong direction are not a good choice for modular quilting because the backing squares as well as the top must be matched. A busy allover print will conceal little errors. Another consideration is whether the fabric will be close in color to the thread with which you are quilting. This is a way to help camouflage any mistakes. Later on, when you have made several quilts, you will see that the quilting pattern on the back is quite wonderful and gives almost as much pleasure as the colorful top.

Do beware of using something too dark on the back. A dark blue can show through a pastel top. It is not often a matter to worry about, but just put a sample of all three layers together before you begin, to see if there is any shadowing effect.

CARING FOR YOUR FABRICS

1. When you bring your fabric home, if it is washable, snip the four corners of the piece to prevent excess fraying, and wash it in the washing machine, each color separately, in warm, soapy water. Use a mild soap such as Ivory because many detergents contain bleach. Keep your eye on the water coming out of the machine to see if it contains a lot of dye. If, as is often the case with strong, dark colors, the rinse water is not clear, wash it again, possibly several times, until all excess dye has been removed and the water is clear. If the water does not become progressively clearer, do not use the fabric. The dye has not been properly set. You may have heard that putting vinegar or salt in the rinse water will set the dye, but it is not true. If the dye was not set properly in the original manufacturing process, you cannot make it happen with home remedies.

2. Never leave an unknown fabric wet in the washing machine and touching another fabric for any length of time. The fabric may crock— that is, leave stains on its damp neighbor. And that unwanted dye is difficult, if not impossible, to remove. But, of course, you may have inadvertently created one of the blotchy tie-dyed effects that other people spend hours trying to achieve—so give it a long hard look before it becomes a dust rag.

3. Line-dry the fabric, or put it through a low or medium cycle on the dryer.

4. Store the washed fabric away from heat and light. These are two factors that strongly affect the wearing qualities of fabrics. It is lovely to have your fabrics arrayed on open shelves around you while you work, and as long as they are used fairly quickly, this practice is fine. However, if you manage to amass a collection so large it cannot possibly be piled up in the open and used quickly, other means must be found to store your fabrics. I store my fabric in numbered boxes (ideally the boxes should be made of inert or acid-free material) and record the amount of fabric and its location in my ''fabric book.'' The fabric book is a loose-leaf binder containing the sort of clear plastic pages used for storing slides or coins (20 small pockets on each page).

After washing and drying my fabric, I take a swatch about $1\frac{1}{2}''$ (4cm) square, glue or staple it onto a small piece of white card, and slip it into one of the pockets. Blank business cards cut in half are ideal. They are available at most stationery stores. On the back of the card is recorded any information about the fabric that you wish to remember, such as the amount, the cost, the date, the place of purchase, and the number of the box in which it is stored (Figure 1-8). The pages are arranged in the book

1-8. This page of the fabric book shows a variety of printed fabric swatches. One card is turned over to show the yardage noted on the back, as well as the box number.

according to color. When I want to use a blue cotton, for instance, I can quickly flip through the pages, see what I have in my collection, find what I want, and get it from its box. (Or go shopping. But I find that I rarely go looking for "that perfect shade of periwinkle blue." Instead, I tend to rearrange the design to make the best use of the fabrics that I already have.)

When the fabric is returned to storage, the amount used is deducted from the amount noted on the back of the card.

OTHER FABRICS

Clearly, cotton is the fabric of choice for most quilters, but that does not mean that other fabrics cannot be employed. I have created and seen beautiful quilts made from silk, velvet, corduroy, and even polyester. Experiment. Make samples with different fabrics before you plunge into a large quilt, keeping in mind the characteristics of various fabrics. Generally, more exotic fabrics should be dry-cleaned, not washed. They are better for more decorative uses such as wall hangings, rather than everyday bed quilts. (See color section.)

Velvet has a nap, which causes the color to change slightly depending on how the light falls on the lengthwise pile of the fabric. If you want the nap always to go the same way, it is best to mark the top of the fabric on each piece. (Sometimes, however, a random nap, or a deliberate rearrangement, will give more interest to a piece.) Velvet stretches and must be carefully pinned, then stitched with an even-feed foot.

Corduroy and **velveteen** also have naps, but are not as stretchy as velvet. They are made of cotton and are hard-wearing and washable.

Satin is easily marked by pins and can't usually be unpicked without leaving marks. It is slippery and it frays. Lining satin pieces and cutting them out with pinking shears helps. Use needles for pinning the pieces together. Satin has no nap, but has directional color differences due to its special weave. Despite these drawbacks, I use it a lot (see color section).

Silk comes in many different weaves and weights and must be treated accordingly. If the dye is fast, it can be washed with care and then ironed dry from a very wet state.

Linen is another natural fiber that is appearing in fashion fabrics again. It is washable and is also best ironed dry from a very wet state. It creases easily.

Velours and other knits stretch and are best used in puff or biscuit quilts where the construction methods take the stress off of the stretchy fabric (see Chapter Nine).

Wool can be bulky and may fray. But the early Amish quilters used fine light wool cloth to wonderful advantage, so again, if you want to use it, experiment first, solve the problems, and then go ahead.

Rayon is reappearing everywhere these days, alone and in blends. It takes dye beautifully and drapes well. But it does have some drawbacks. It is slippery to work with and so should be lined, and it frays a lot so it should be cut with pinking shears. It is more susceptible to abrasion than other fabrics, but washes well.

Ramie and other exotic fabrics, some natural and some man-made, are also making their way into dress-weight fabrics. I suggest you approach them with caution and experiment with them first to discover their handling characteristics and washability before using them in a large project.

THE WORK STATION

As in any other job, the place where you actually do your sewing contributes greatly to your success. Many of you will not have a lot of space in which to work, but if it can be set up so it is comfortable and convenient, you will feel like working there more often, and more beautiful quilts will be the result.

My area is set up in a "U" configuration, with my sewing maching and ironing board on either side of a large work table. The table can support a big piece of work in the final stages of construction. It is also the place where I do all my designing, cutting, and pinning.

Be sure your light is good. If it needs improving, you can probably clamp an inexpensive gooseneck lamp to the table and guide it to the area where you are working.

A swivel chair is one of the keys to efficiency. It allows you to turn and move easily between the sewing machine, the ironing board, and the work table for successive steps in the sewing process. The ironing board can easily be adjusted to the height of the table and the sewing machine. You can also adjust the seat of the chair to a comfortable height. I have adjusted mine so that the ironing board, table, and sewing machine are at the level of my waist when I am sitting.

If speed is really a concern (it shouldn't be—efficiency is a better aim), don't cut and snip and tidy your work as you go along. Wait until you have to. Then you can usually snip threads and trim seams with the rotary cutter in one movement. Pile up stitching and pressing to do all at once. Your work pace and system will depend on whether your rewards come from the slow, methodical growth of a work made of hundreds of tiny steps or from the great exciting splash of the finished work.

By checking measurements and corner joins as you go, you can prevent big disasters later. And remember that making a quilt is akin to painting a room—it's all in the preparation. Accurate cutting, careful pressing, precise pinning and stitching, though unseen, will give wonderful results. And each piece is a challenge. The peculiarities of the pattern or the characteristics of the fabric will make it different from other things you have done and give you joy when it is completed successfully. Now, let's design your quilt.

The Black and Yellow Quilt, 60″ × 60″ (150cm × 150cm), Pat Cairns, 1987. This quilt, made of only two strongly contrasting colors, shows the effectiveness of counterchange in creating pattern. Photographer, Barbara Cohen; owner, Pat Cairns.

The Road to Expo, 45″ × 45″ (115cm × 115cm), Pat Cairns, 1990. This quilt illustrates all the techniques needed to create a myriad of patterns. With only three colors—light, medium, and dark—the combinations are endless. Photographer, Barbara Cohen; owner, Pat Cairns.

Evergreen Playground, 75" × 95" (190cm × 240cm), Pat Cairns, 1982. More than one thousand puffs of many different fabrics combine to give a feeling of the dominant blues and greens of the Pacific Northwest. Photographer, Pat Cairns; owner, Elaine Cairns.

Rainforest I, 87" × 87" (220cm × 220cm), Jean Affleck, 1982. This clever design made of multistrips cut into triangles and trapezoids, has an almost invisible lattice worked into the design, making construction quite simple. Photographer, Pat Cairns; owner, Carolyn Affleck.

Baby Blanket, 42" × 48" (105cm × 120cm), Wendy Lewington Coulter, 1987. This piece uses the strong lines of machine appliqué to great effect. The border has strip piecing with bright glittery fabrics. Photographer, Brenda Hemsing; owner, Claire Coulter.

Traffic Jam? 34" × 62" (85cm × 155cm), Pat Cairns, 1988. Granville Island, where I have my studio, has a chronic traffic problem, with too many cars on twisty one-way streets. I used the colors of traffic signals to make a quilt expressing the every-which-wayness of city traffic. Photographer, Pat Cairns; owner, Paul Tennant.

Cabbagetown Concentrics, 54" × 54" (135cm × 135cm), Pat Cairns, 1990. Careful attention to value in a narrow color range results in flickering movement across slightly interrupted pale and dark squares. Photographer, Barbara Cohen; owners, Rick and Liora Salter.

Disappearing Forest, 72" × 82" (180cm × 205cm), Louise Slobodan, 1987. The artist has used her own silk screened images to create the changing patterns in this quilt, which is a straight set block construction. Photographer, Tony Redpath; owner, Thomas Ecker.

View to the West, 112" × 112" (285cm × 285cm), Pat Cairns, 1987. This piece gained its inspiration when I stood, one lovely summer evening, on an apartment balcony eighteen stories up and saw the sun set gloriously over the mountains and the sea. Photographer, Ingrid Yuille; owners, Pat and Alan Cairns.

Wildly Red, 40" × 57.5" (100cm × 145cm), Pat Cairns, 1990. This piece uses the same pattern as *Stepping Stones,* but I decided to disrupt it by moving the lights and darks around, using only my favorite color—red—with a little of this and a little of that! Photographer, Pat Cairns; owner, Pat Cairns.

Cinderella, 39" × 48" (100cm × 120cm), Jeannie Kamins, 1986. Jeannie uses every kind of fabric in her machine appliqué. Often the most unlikely fabrics are the most appropriate. The strong, heavy black lines around the figures help simplify and clarify her work. Photographer, Jeannie Kamins; owner, Sunnyhill Hospital, Vancouver.

Expo Sky Sites maquette, 16" × 18" (40cm × 45cm), Pat Cairns, 1985. After this maquette was presented to a designer and accepted, I made a large quilt 98" × 108" (245cm × 270cm) in nine sections, using applied binding on the back, as described in Chapter Six. It was hung in the Folklife Pavilion at the Expo '86 World's Fair in Vancouver, Canada. Photographer, Robert Kezire; owner, Pat Cairns.

The Stars Are Coming Out, 104" × 116" (265cm × 295cm), Pat Cairns, 1990. When deciding on color placement for this quilt, I ignored the pattern in the sense that I made no attempt to make it easily readable. Color movement dominates. Photographer, Barbara Cohen; owner, Gil Hardman.

Blue Stars for Betty, 22" × 43" (55cm × 110cm), Pat Cairns, 1989. This commission was a challenge— to make an interesting design with a very small (for a quilter that is!) format. The solution was in moving around the stars, placing them asymmetrically and incompletely. Photographer, Pat Cairns; owner, Betty Holden.

In Memorium, 48.5" × 42" (125cm × 105cm), Nerida Benson Mandl, 1988. Hand quilted. Nerida made this lovely, simply patterned, rainbow-like quilt with "blackbirds" on it after her mother died. She often uses words, sometimes poetry, on her quilts, which gives a special personal quality to the works. The inscription is "I have heard the mavis singing her lovesong to the morn." Her mother's name was Mavis, which means blackbird. Photographer, Barbara Cohen; owner, Nerida Benson Mandl.

Stepping Stones, 63" × 93" (160cm × 235cm), Pat Cairns, 1989. Fairly traditional coloring was used in this piece, inspired by a picture of an old quilt made of four-patch and half-square triangle units. I made the quilt in sections with applied back binding. Photographer, Barbara Cohen; owner, Pat Cairns.

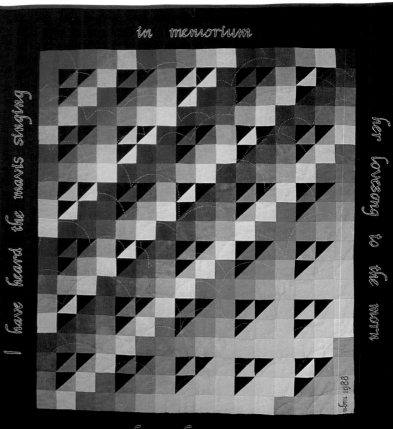

CHAPTER TWO

How to Design a Quilt

"Seems my mind just couldn't quit planning patterns and colors, and the piecing, the sewing with the needle comforted me."

(from The Quilters, by Patricia Cooper and Norma Bradley Buferd)

THE MODULES

A quilt has three parts—a decorative top, a thicker filling, and a backing fabric, all held together by stitching. The emphasis in the methods of quiltmaking discussed in this book is on a modular approach. This means that the quilt sandwich is not quilted in one large piece. Rather, it is divided into sections, or modules, which are quilted through the three layers before they are joined together to make the complete quilt.

After you have decided on the design for your quilt top, assess it to see how the pattern can be broken up into modules that will be quilted, by hand or machine, before being joined to the other modules to complete the quilt. A module can be a traditional quilt block, a strip running the width or length of the quilt, or any other workable portion. There are very few designs that cannot be constructed using one of the methods outlined in this book. The whole cloth quilt is an obvious exception. There are other designs, such as the Lone Star, which in theory could be made in modules, but in practice the modular approach is more difficult than a traditional one.

What you want is to break up the large quilt surface into units that are more manageable in the sewing machine, are easier to work with, and are more portable. A module can be a whole baby quilt or a section of a large quilt. A rough dimension that I keep in mind when thinking about dividing up a design for machine quilting is 25" (65cm) square. A module of this size goes under the sewing machine needle easily and is not large enough or heavy enough to be cumbersome. If you are interested in doing some complex quilting that requires the block to be turned often, single blocks are the best modules. The object is to find a module that is manageable and that suits your practical considerations and your aesthetic sensibilities (that is, the divisions of the quilt from the back look planned and balanced, not hodgepodge).

Although I am going to tell you a lot about construction, I don't want ease of construction to be your only consideration when making a quilt. I do want the major consideration to be a design you have made your own in some way. You have chosen or invented the pattern, the size you wish to make it, the set, the borders, and the fabric colors and have made every other artistic decision involved in making a quilt. Knowledge of the wide range of construction methods available will help you make these decisions. You should not have to buy a pattern book because you can make your own pattern to suit your needs exactly.

The pretext some people give for making quilts is that they are warm, functional bed covers, but the real reason they make a quilt is that it is a beautiful object. What makes it beautiful is the top, so we will begin our discussion of the parts of the quilt with the top.

PIECED TOPS

Many quilt tops are made of patchwork. This involves cutting out geometric shapes such as squares, triangles, circles, and other more complex shapes, then stitching them together to form a pattern. Traditionally, each patch was cut separately and then hand sewn to other patches to make a block. Newer methods, which make use of the sewing machine in combination with various cutting devices, greatly speed up the process.

THE BLOCK

Quilt blocks are made up of smaller units. Usually blocks can be divided into four, nine, or sixteen sections (see Figures 2-1, 2-2, and 2-3). These sections are made first (sometimes of more than one patch) and joined to each other to make larger units or the whole quilt.

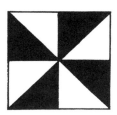

2-1. The four-patch block shown here is made of half-square triangle units. It can be made of plain or printed fabric. (See page 50 to make these units.)

2-2. A nine-patch block is made of nine units of equal size. This example uses five printed fabric units and four half-square triangle units.

2-3. A sixteen-patch block may seem complex, but it is made from very simple units. Four plain fabric units, four printed fabric units, and eight half-square triangle units have been used to make this design.

After you have looked at a number of quilts and are able to see the repeat patterns, you can decide if a particular quilt can be made using assembly-line piecing methods. Look for such things as squares, rectangles, and half-square triangles where color sequences repeat. Avoid curved seams and geometric shapes such as parallelograms and rhomboids unless you see that these shapes can be broken into squares, right-angle triangles, or rectangles. Some patterns that contain geometric shapes with acute angles, such as Mariner's Compass, and those with equilateral triangles, such as Thousands of Pyramids, cannot be made with these methods.

2-4. The Road to Expo Block. This is a four-patch block, but this time two of the four "patches" are themselves four-patch units, and the other two are half-square triangle units, each composed of a light and a dark right-angle triangle.

2-5. Straight set.

Please note that I am not counseling you to avoid such patterns, but if you do use them, employ the traditional methods and enjoy both the method and the results.

The block chosen to illustrate our modular approach is made up of four units: two four-patches and two half-square triangle units (see Figure 2-4). It is called the *Road to Expo* block.

THE SET

The set is the arrangement of blocks, which creates the overall pattern of the quilt. There are many ways quilts can be set using an identical block. You will see in Figures 2-5 through 2-15 what dramatically different designs can be created with a change in the set. In most of these figures, you can find the *Road to Expo* block in the upper left-hand corner—look to see how it is repeated in different ways.

Straight set. In the simplest arrangement identical blocks are placed next to each other in rows. When these rows are repeated, a powerful design can emerge (Figure 2-5).

Alternating blocks. To create a checkerboard effect, place plain blocks between two pieced or appliquéd blocks (Figure 2-6).

2-6. The addition of alternating plain blocks.

Complicated patterns can be created using only two different blocks. See Figures 2-7 and 2-8, in which a simple Pinwheel block is set next to the Road to Expo block to create two different designs.

2-7. Alternating two blocks, The Road to Expo and Pinwheel, to form a new pattern.

2-8. Our illustrator, Carolyn Affleck, couldn't resist making her own design with the same two blocks!

Lattice strips. Lattices are used not only to join modules (see Chapter Four), but also as a design element. Lattices can vary in width, from very narrow to about 4" (10cm). They can be plain or decoratively pieced. Depending on the way you color the lattice, it can frame each block, or it can meld into the design and become almost invisible (see Figures 2-9 through 2-11 and Rainforest I in the color section).

2-9. Lattice strips are used to frame and float the block.

2-10. Here the lattices meld into the block and cause only certain parts of it to float.

Corner blocks can be incorporated into a lattice design, as was done in the Road to Expo quilt. To use them, join the blocks into rows with

2-11. Turned Road to Expo blocks with lattice strips.

2-12. Effective use of corner blocks with a straight set design.

2-15. Turned blocks set on point. Diagonals always seem to give life to a design.

short lattices, and incorporate the corner blocks into the long lattice strips that join the rows together. Figure 2-12 shows another example.

Turned blocks. Look at Figures 2-11, 2-13, and 2-14 to see what can happen when blocks set next to each other are turned in various ways before joining. By turning blocks, you can change the overall pattern of the quilt dramatically.

2-13. A turned block set that gives a central point of interest to the design.

2-14. These turned blocks, set without lattices, give strong up and down movement to the design.

Diagonal sets. When blocks are set on point as in Figures 2-6, 2-9, and 2-15, they are joined in rows that go diagonally across the quilt surface, making them appear as diamonds, rather than squares.

As you can see, you have many effective design tools at your disposal. You can manipulate the two simple elements of a pieced top—the block and the set—in an endless variety of ways.

THE SIZE

Usually when you make a quilt, you have in mind a specific use for it and a rough idea of the size you want it to be. If the quilt is to go on a bed, you need to measure the bed to determine the length and width required for the quilt. The length can include a pillow tuck, and the width should take into account how far down the sides of the bed you want the quilt to hang. With this information you can begin to consider block size, use and width of lattices, if any, and borders.

If, for instance, we use the Road to Expo block in an 8″ (20cm) size, the quilt will have to measure some multiple of 8″ (20cm), exclusive of borders and lattices. A bit of experimentation with the widths of borders or lattices will probably give dimensions close to the ideal ones with which you began.

If more drastic measures are necessary (as when altering a single bed design to that of a queen-size bed), you may want to change the block size or number of pattern repeats. These are big changes. Eight 8″

(20cm) blocks give a length of 64″ (160cm) while eight 9″ (25cm) blocks are 72″ (200cm) long. Sometimes such changes disrupt the relationship of the block size to the whole quilt design. By that I mean that sometimes a block can be enlarged to the point where the whole design becomes rather bland and uninteresting. There are not enough repeats to make the quilt a well-designed whole. The quilt may be easy to make because the pieces required are few and large, but the end result will not be worth it.

You can, of course, go in the other direction and make the pieces so tiny that the design takes forever to make; try to find the right balance between block size and finished quilt. Looking at quilts, both old and new, and lots of pictures of them in books will help you gain the knowledge you need to make these decisions.

Your design will require an even or uneven number of repeats. For instance, Figure 2-13 needs an even number of blocks while Figure 2-6 requires an uneven number for balance. To check, place a piece of paper over one row of blocks in each of these designs and see how the balance is disrupted. The designs seem unfinished, not at rest. Adding blocks in pairs can make a considerable difference to the size of the quilt.

THE QUILTING LINE

The machine quilting line is a strong design element. Most of the time I use it to outline the piecing I have done, stitching on top of the seam lines that join the pieces together. This is called **stitching-in-the-ditch.** If you want the quilting to create a secondary pattern, take care to choose a design that enhances rather than fights the pieced design.

WAYS TO DESIGN A QUILT

Most quilts are made up of blocks. The blocks you choose, whether traditional or original, and their sets and colors are what make your quilt a unique and wonderful creation. To help you achieve this special expression of your creativity, I will outline some methods I find helpful in my own work.

USE A PHOTOCOPY MACHINE

Choose a block or blocks that you would like to work with from the many books that illustrate quilt patterns and blocks. The bibliography lists several books you can look for in the library or your local quilt shop. It is good to build your own collection of books because the design process requires time and thought. Choose books with clear and precise drawings.

Take a piece of graph paper and a pen you like, and draw a few blocks. I don't bother with a ruler at this stage. The very act of putting down these lines freehand helps you to see and feel the units from which the block is constructed and to understand how they go together.

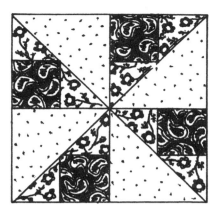

After you have decided on one or two blocks as a starting point, draw a typing-paper-sized page full of them, close together (but not too small), using all the space you can. Then go and photocopy the page several times so that you have 20 to 30 blocks to work with. Cut the blocks apart and begin to arrange them in various sets. When you have found a set or two that you think is interesting, glue-stick the arrangements of the blocks onto a backing paper and photocopy the pages several times. Now you can get out your colored pencils or felt-tip pens and begin to experiment with color. This method is rough—the crayons can only approximate the colors of fabrics—but it gives you an idea of the way the whole quilt could look when you are finished. It helps you discover how lights and darks can affect the design. Figure 2-16 shows how different one block can look when its lights and darks are moved around.

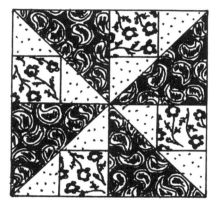

FABRIC SKETCHES

The best way to discover how a quilt will look is to take the actual fabrics that will be used in the quilt and make a mock-up or maquette. This is the model artists often make before executing a large piece of work. It helps the artist solve any problems involved in such an endeavor before beginning work. A quilt is certainly a large enough and serious enough project to warrant a maquette. I developed this method to help me understand what my finished pieces would look like. I began to realize that the essence of my work is color and its movement across the surface of a simple pattern. Pencil and paint colors do not translate readily into fabrics.

TO MAKE A MOCK-UP AS A COLOR EXERCISE

1. Gather and press small pieces of the fabrics you are considering for your design.

2. Take a piece of graph paper of standard typing paper size and cut an 8″ (20cm) square or a rectangle 8″ × 10″ (20cm × 25cm) from it, then mount it with glue-stick to a backing of thin white cardboard. This forms a stiffened grid base with a plain white border on which you can experiment with color placement.

3. Put each pressed piece of fabric on top of a separate piece of graph paper, and cut some 1″ (2cm) squares. Or if you prefer, cut the little squares with the rotary cutter, self-healing mat, and plastic ruler.

2-16. Three ways to place the same fabrics in the same block.

4. Begin placing the squares on the prepared background in various configurations. Try grading lights and darks from the center out, from top to bottom, diagonally, or from side to side. You will quickly see the effect one color has on another when they are placed side by side. I suggest you use small squares to do this exercise because the pattern takes over if more complex shapes are used. If you want more subtlety or gradation,

however, cut some of the squares into rectangles and half-square triangles and use them that way.

5. To get the best results from these exercises, do them in a playful, relaxed manner. Put outrageous things together. Use strong contrasts, gradual color changes, all sorts of things. You are not committing to actually make the designs, just to find out what happens when certain colors are put together.

6. When you have evolved a color placement that you want to keep, apply glue-stick to the *graph paper backing,* not to the fabric. Then you can easily affix the small pieces of fabric to the backing.

TO MAKE A MAQUETTE FOR A LARGE PIECE

Glue-stick is only a temporary adhesive. When I am making a maquette for a commissioned piece, I want it to be longer lasting, so I have devised a slightly different method for use in these circumstances.

Usually the maquette will be considerably larger than the small color sketches described above, so I begin with larger sheets of graph paper, and larger, stiffer backing card. I often use mat board for this. Scale doesn't really matter. Just make sure the fabric pieces you work with are not so tiny as to drive you mad or blind in the process. I think $\frac{1}{2}$″ (1cm) squares are the absolute minimum for a sane life. For instance, the block shown in Figure 2-17 (which is a schematic representation of the blocks shown in Figure 2-16) could have each of its 16 components represented by 1″ (2cm) or $\frac{1}{2}$″ (1cm) squares on your maquette, regardless of whether the finished block is to be 8″ (20cm) or 12″ (30cm) square.

1. Draw out your design on graph paper twice.

2. Stiffen sample pieces approximately 8″ × 10″ (20cm × 25cm) of the fabrics you are considering for the design. Using spray starch and a dry iron produces a nice stiff fabric that is easy to cut and to move around in the design.

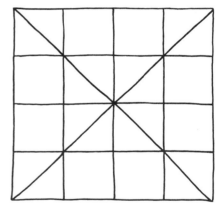

2-17. Schematic drawing for Figure 2-16.

3. With a rotary cutter, board, and ruler, cut your stiffened fabrics into the small pieces to be used in the design.

4. Arrange these pieces on one copy of the design. When you are satisfied with the arrangement, take the second drawing and tape it with removable tape to a firm surface, such as a table or a drawing board.

5. Cover the design area of the paper with strips of double-sided tape, available in art, hardware, or office supply stores. Starting from the bottom, peel off the protection from one row of tape and transfer the pieces of colored cloth from the design arrangment that you have just made to the one covered with sticky tape. Do this carefully (tweezers help), one row at a time, and you will soon have a handsome miniature

of the quilt you intend to make. (See the Expo Sky Sites maquette in the color section.)

If you are one of those who thinks, as I do, that color and its placement is one of the most exciting things about quiltmaking, almost any repeat design will allow you to create wonderful quilts. But choose a pattern that is not too complex to construct. The emphasis should be on design and color, not on virtuoso sewing. The rest of this book will give you all the techniques you need to put the quilt together beautifully and well.

ANOTHER KIND OF FABRIC BOOK

From each piece of fabric that I contemplate using to make a maquette, I cut and stiffen a piece about 8" × 10" (20cm × 25cm). After the maquette is finished, the unused portions of these pieces are stored in yet another fabric book (Figure 2-18). Each plastic page in this book

2-18. Another kind of fabric book, in which I store small pieces of stiffened fabric, ready for use in designing a maquette.

holds a sheet of typing paper (for background). I use a page holder for each of my numbered boxes of fabric. Thus many pieces can be stored together and are ready for the next design session. I find I have favorite fabrics I use over and over until they are gone.

MIRROR MAGIC

For Jean, whose designs were composed in a different way than mine, another type of fabric mock-up proved useful.

1. Draw and then photocopy several times the block you are considering. Make the drawing larger, about 4–6" (10–15cm) square, or thereabouts—not full-size, but large enough to construct easily.

2. From your stock of small starched pieces of fabric, cut squares and triangles to fit one drawing.

3. Glue-stick the fabric into place on the paper.

4. If the first arrangement doesn't please you, try another color arrangement on a second photocopy of the drawing. Continue, remembering to be playful—you are learning a lot and not wasting anything—these fabric pieces are very tiny.

5. Interesting and unexpected shapes often occur when a block is repeated. To see how your design will look in repeat without further cutting and gluing, find two mirrors and place them upright and at 90° angles at one corner of the block (Figure 2-19). Instantly you will see

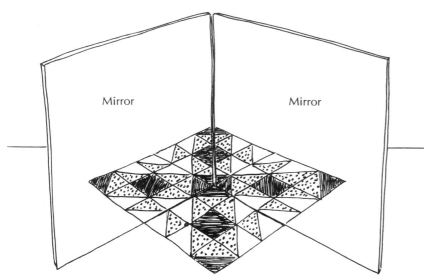

2-19. Two mirrors placed at right angles next to the corner of a symmetrical block to show what a four-block repeat would look like.

what a four-block repeat will look like. (The block alone is shown in Figure 2-20.) But note that the mirror will not show a straight set unless the chosen block is perfectly symmetrical. Mirrors give reverse images.

2-20. The block used in Figure 2-19.

USING FULL-SIZE FABRIC PIECES

When you have decided on the block you will use to construct the quilt, your colors, and perhaps the set, cut out enough full-size pieces for about four blocks. Arrange them on a white background. (I have a large white flannelette sheet stapled over wallboard on my studio wall. The wallboard was painted before the sheet was stretched over it to keep the soft, thick, porous wallboard from crumbling away when pins are repeatedly stuck into it.) Stand back from the arrangement to see how the colors actually work together. To get even more distance from the project, look through the wrong end of binoculars, which will act as a reducing lens. If the arrangement doesn't suit you, try transposing the colors in some way. Use darks where the lights are now. Make more contrast or less in various areas. These considerations are well worth making here with only four blocks of fabric cut out, rather than the many needed to complete a full-sized quilt.

COLOR—THE QUILTER'S BEST TOOL

Color choice is subjective and personal. The objective in using the design tools above is to help you become more sensitive to color. Your awareness will improve with practice. Everyone makes design and color decisions every day. Putting your clothes on in the morning, setting the table, or arranging flowers all require looking at colors and their relationship to each other.

One way you can make a success of your first quilt is to limit your palette to two colors of high contrast—one dark and one light. If this idea appeals to you, look at old red-and-white or blue-and-white quilts (these are often illustrated in quilt books). You will quickly see how dramatic they can be.

In **counterchange** two colors are reversed in adjacent identical units (Figure 2-21). Designs called Robbing Peter to Pay Paul use this technique. An example of counterchange is shown in The Black and Yellow Quilt (see color section). The design is the same as in Figure 2-21, but a border has been added.

Do keep in mind that it is the contrast in the value of the colors placed next to each other which allows you to read the pattern made by the patches. Even such strongly contrasting colors as red and green will not create a readable pattern if they are both of the same degree of lightness and darkness.

In my piece Wildly Red (see color section) I used my knowlege of the essential role of value in creating a design that deliberately disrupts the clarity of the pattern. In some areas patches close in value were set next to each other to interrupt the eye as it tries to follow the pattern and to make the viewer look again, to notice the textures and the wonderful variety of reds and near-reds that there are.

Blocks do not all have to be colored identically. For instance, if you are using green and blue, begin lightening some blue areas and darkening some green ones. Try to get a sense of movement across the quilt. (See The Stars Are Coming Out in the color section.) Depending on your point of view, quilts that use the same color scheme in the same places in every block can be static or serene.

You can create a rich surface by using values of one color or a group of analogous colors—those that touch one another on the color wheel and could be said to be a family, such as green, yellow-green, and blue-green. Perhaps after working on a fabric sketch using a variety of values

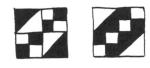

2-21. Counterchange.

of one color or an analogous grouping, you will still feel something is missing, that it lacks life. Try adding a touch of the complementary color (the opposite one on the color wheel, Figure 2-22).

Black is a useful noncolor. It will not change the relationship between the colors you have chosen, but provides a background that will increase their brilliance. This is known as the jewel effect. (See Rainforest I in the color section.) White was often used as the background color in older, traditional quilts and insured that there was a light value to contrast with the other colors, just as black now often provides the darkest of dark values for modern quilters who have been influenced by Amish quilts.

What will become clear to you, after even a short time playing with tiny pieces of fabric and making mock-ups, is that your perception of color is directly influenced by the colors that surround it.

As you make more quilts, you will become a fabric collector, too. Often all the inspiration you need is contained in your boxes of fabric. Play with the fabrics a bit. By this I mean suspend all the rules you have learned about what colors *should* go into a quilt and see what happens when you juggle things. Essentially I am telling you to use intuitive methods of learning about colors and not to worry about the rules found in artists' handbooks. These are useful sometimes, but should be resorted to only occasionally as a reference tool. I include below a short description of the terms used in books on color so that if you must, you can work your way through them.

The feel and look of fabrics can never quite be captured on paper with any coloring implements. I like to work directly with the fabric because the design and construction of the quilt are really parts of one continuous process. When we make quilts, we make something we want to last a long time. Usually, we want the quilt to express love and affection, and so our emotions are naturally involved. Therefore we must allow the fabrics and the colors to say things to us as we manipulate them.

When you are looking at things—quilts, glossy magazines, paintings, displays in department stores—think about them in terms of color. Why do you like some and not others? Into your idea file can go photographs, bits of wallpapers, wrapping paper, old birthday cards—anything you like in terms of color and shape. Then, when you are struggling to get a quilt started, you can go back and look at all these things and find inspiration.

THE COLOR WHEEL

Figure 2-22 shows you how the colors are arranged on a color wheel. There are three **primary colors**—red, yellow, and blue—which divide the circle into thirds. All other colors are mixed from these three. The **secondary colors**—orange, green, and purple—fall between the primary colors and are made by combining two of them. Red + yellow makes orange, yellow + blue makes green, and blue + red makes purple. **Tertiary colors** come from the combination of a primary color and a secondary color and take the name of the combination, such as yellow-green, or red-orange.

Hue is the color name, such as red, blue, or green.

Value is the degree of lightness or darkness. Dark values have black added to them and are called **shades.** Light values have white added and are called **tints.** Contrast in value establishes the pattern of the quilt.

Intensity is the purity or saturation of a color. Adding gray reduces the intensity of a hue and produces a **tone.**

Warm colors are those on the orange side of the color wheel. They tend to advance. **Cool** colors, on the blue side, tend to recede.

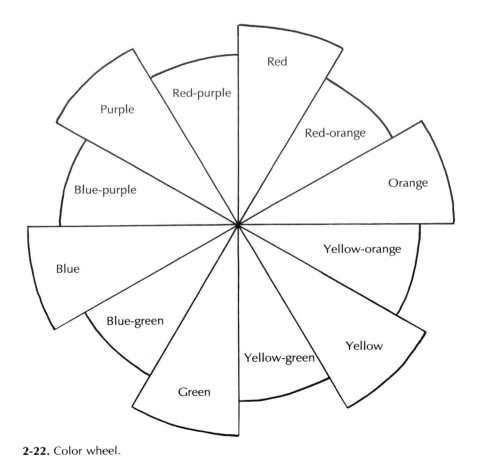

2-22. Color wheel.

TYPES OF COLOR SCHEMES

If you feel you need a bit of structure to your color experimentation, try some of the color arrangements described below when you are doing fabric mock-up exercises.

Monochromatic refers to a group of fabrics of many shades, tints, tones (and sometimes textures) of a single color. For example, a quilt might be done all in green but with fabrics that are light, dark, print, velvet, and silk.

Complementary colors are opposite each other on the color wheel, such as red and green, yellow and purple, and orange and blue. Complementary colors need not be used pure or in equal quantities. Often just a touch of the complement will enhance the design.

Analogous colors lie next to each other on the color wheel, such as red, orange, and yellow. Again, the strength of each color and the amount used should differ and create variety.

NUMBER OF COLORS

The **two-color scheme** is one of the best and certainly the easiest to begin with. High contrast is important and can create dramatic designs.

For a **three-color scheme**, be sure there are light, dark, and medium values in the fabrics you use and that they are placed carefully, perhaps to emphasize the part of the design you like best.

Quilts of **many colors**, into which category fall such things as scrap quilts, charm quilts, and crazy quilts, along with many other types, seem best when the fabrics and values are carefully arranged to give light and dark areas, or some repeated motif or theme.

USING PRINTED FABRICS WHEN CREATING A COLOR SCHEME

Quilters have always loved and used printed fabrics in their work. But sometimes prints can pose a problem when you are making a color statement. The difficulty can arise when the print itself is composed of highly contrasting elements, such as a red flower on a white background. It is much easier to use a red flower with a pink background. Most of the prints I use appear from a distance as one color, and then reveal themselves on closer inspection.

Of course, you can use highly contrasting prints, but usually you need several in a design, which then can become very busy and lack pattern design. But that, too, is a style of the 1990s, so if you like it, do it!

PART II
PUTTING IT ALL TOGETHER

CHAPTER THREE

Cutting and Piecing the Blocks

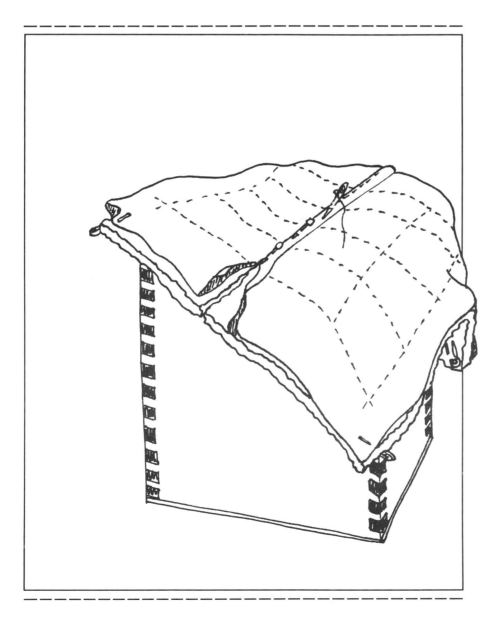

In Chapters Three and Four we will construct, using the modular approach, a small quilt called the Road to Expo (Figure 3-1). The design

3-1. The Road to Expo quilt.

3-2. The four-patch block.

3-3. The half-square triangle block.

divides easily into modules, incorporates lattice strips with corner blocks, and has a double border. While the design of the finished quilt appears complicated, it is not difficult to make. Sixteen 8" (20cm) square blocks (Figures 3-2 and 3-3) are sewn together to make each of four modules. The modules are then quilted and joined to each other with lattice strips and corner blocks. Finally, the multiple border is added. The border has the wonderful Never-Fail Mitered Corner (see Chapter Four).

The finished quilt is 45" (112cm) square. But any quilt, of any size, large or small, can be constructed with these methods. (See the color section for lots of examples.)

FIGURING YARDAGE AND CUTTING DIAGRAMS

For those of you who make clothes, cutting diagrams are like the ones you receive in a commercial pattern. They are like maps, really, of how best to cut the pieces required from the least amount of fabric. You need to make one for each fabric in the design. I have used 45" (115cm) wide fabric, but if you have another width, such as 36" (90cm) or 60" (150cm), remember to take that fact into consideration. All seam allowances have been included in the pieces being diagramed ($\frac{1}{2}$" or 1cm).

The fabric may shrink when it is washed. Assume in your diagrams that 45" (115cm) fabric will measure only 43" (110cm) after washing. Even the most skilled and experienced quilters occasionally make cutting errors or discover unexpected flaws in the fabric that must be compensated for, so add a few inches or centimeters to the length when deciding how much fabric to buy.

BORDERS

The border strips will be the longest pieces of fabric you will need, and they look best if they are cut in one piece. If joining is necessary, and it will be at times, a bias join is less noticeable than one on the straight of the grain (see Figures 3-4 and 3-5.)

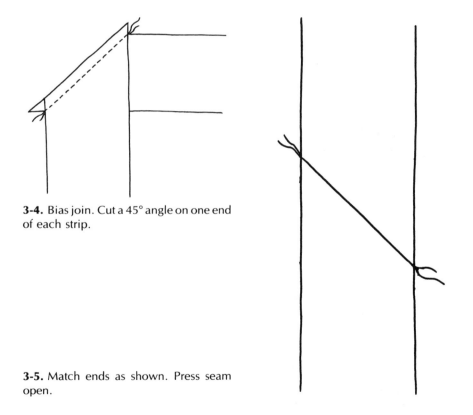

3-4. Bias join. Cut a 45° angle on one end of each strip.

3-5. Match ends as shown. Press seam open.

Cut the borders on the lengthwise grain of the fabric. There is less stretch than from selvage to selvage. To find the length of the border strips needed, add together the following (see Figure 3-6):

1. The length of the modules

2. The width of the lattices

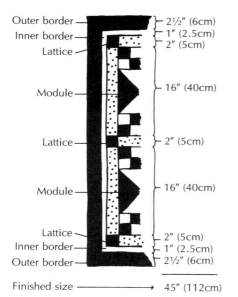

Outer border — 2½" (6cm)
Inner border — 1" (2.5cm)
Lattice — 2" (5cm)

Module — 16" (40cm)

Lattice — 2" (5cm)

Module — 16" (40cm)

Lattice — 2" (5cm)
Inner border — 1" (2.5cm)
Outer border — 2½" (6cm)

Finished size ———————→ 45" (112cm)

3-6. Add these measurements together to get the length, and add 1" (2cm) for seam allowances plus 2" (5cm) for error.

3-7. Extended module.

3. The top and bottom border widths

4. The seam allowances of the border itself

5. A little extra, about 2" (5cm).

For the Road to Expo quilt you will make a border out of two fabrics, and it will have a double mitered corner. You will need four strips of each of the two colors. The light inner border strip will be 1" (2.5cm) when finished, with ½" (1cm) seam allowances on each side. The length is calculated as in Figure 3-6, but excluding the outside dark border.

When the dark outside border is added with a 2½" (6cm) finished width, the total width of the border becomes 3½" (8.5cm). To make the double mitered border, the dark outside fabric is cut from strips 7" (16.5cm) wide. After the mitered corners are made, the border is folded over to the back of the quilt to cover the batting.

BACKING

Choose your backing fabric so that it contributes to the aesthetic whole of the piece. You can use the same fabric in parts of the top or in the border.

Cut the backing larger than the finished dimensions of the module by at least 2" (5cm). The amount will vary, depending on the part of the quilt you are backing. The modules around the edge of the quilt often include the border, whereas central ones do not.

The Road to Expo quilt is assembled from four modules, each 16" (40cm) square when finished. But the backing squares are cut for an *extended module* (Figure 3-7). This means (in this case) that two pieces of lattice and a corner block have been added around the two outside edges of the module. Borders will be added along these two edges also, so cut the backing squares 22½" × 22½" (57.5cm × 57.5cm), which is one-half the width of your 45" (115cm) wide fabric.

The reason the backing fabric is cut larger than the pieced top is that it makes the layering process in the next stage much easier. If the backing and the top are the same size, it can be difficult to get them properly positioned with a layer of batting in between. (But if your fabric has shrunk a bit widthwise, don't worry in this case. Don't buy extra fabric to get exactly 22½". The backing is trimmed in a later step. Just get as close to this measurement as your fabric will allow.)

LATTICES

The lattices, made of medium-value fabric, join the four modules together. The width of the lattice is 2" (5cm) finished and the length of each 16" (40cm). When the seam allowances are included, the lattices are cut from 3" (7cm) strips and are 17" (42cm) long. Nine corner blocks, each 3" (7cm) square, of the dark fabric are used in this design.

THE PIECED TOP—MULTIPLE PIECING

Rather than use templates to cut squares and triangles, I sew strips of fabric together lengthwise to make a **multistrip.** I then cut the multistrip crosswise to produce **segments.** These components are recombined to produce a **unit,** which may be either a block or a portion of a block.

Because multiple piecing techniques are so quick, plan a few extra units to make a practice block or module and to allow for errors and imperfections in the cutting and piecing. You may use a little more fabric working this way, but you spend less time correcting imperfect joins and cuts.

TOTAL FABRIC REQUIREMENTS FOR THE ROAD TO EXPO QUILT

Light fabric	1¼ yards (1.2m)
Medium fabric	2 yards (1.8m)
Dark fabric	2¼ yards (2m)

Light Fabric

Following Figure 3-8, cut from this fabric:

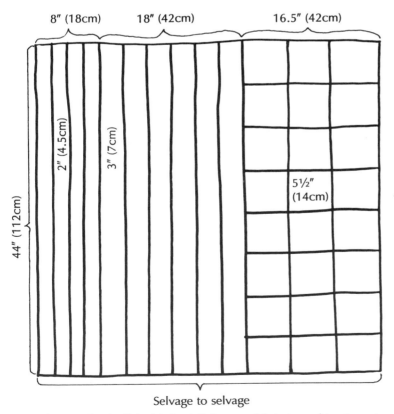

3-8. Cutting diagram for the light fabric. A little more fabric is used to give extra units when cutting each fabric.

1. Four inside borders, 2″ × 44″ (4.5cm × 112cm).

2. Six strips to make four-patch units, 3″ × 44″ (7cm × 112cm).

3. A rectangle 16.5″ × 44″ (42cm × 112cm) for the half-square triangle units.

Medium Fabric

Following Figure 3-9, cut from this fabric:

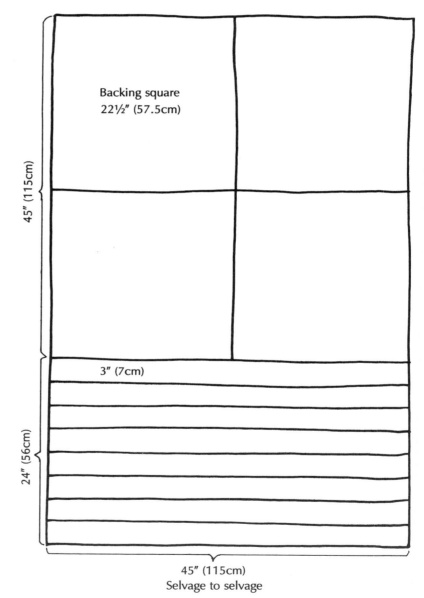

3-9. Cutting diagram for the medium fabric.

1. Four squares 22½″ × 22½″ (57.5cm × 57.5cm) for the backing.

2. Eight strips 3″ × 45″ (7cm × 115cm), which is the full width of the fabric. From these strips you will cut one long back lattice 3″ × 39″ (7cm × 102cm); two short back lattices 3″ × 19″ (7cm × 47cm); twelve short front lattices 3″ × 17″ (7cm × 42cm).

Dark Fabric

Following Figure 3-10, cut from this fabric:

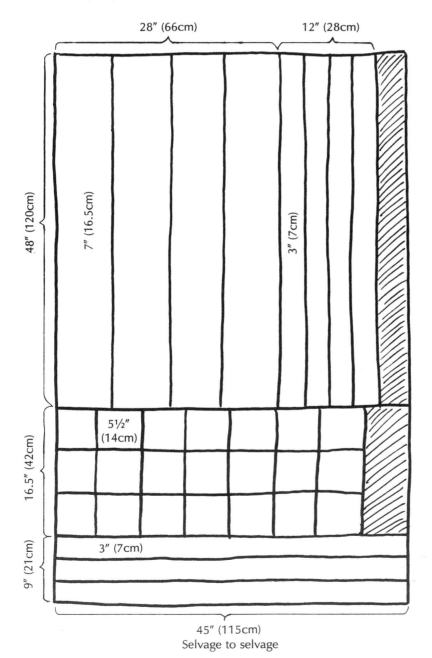

3-10. Cutting diagram for the dark fabric.

1. Four outside borders 7" × 48" (16.5 cm × 120cm). These dark strips make the double border which folds over the batting to the back 3.5" (8.5cm).

2. Seven strips 3" × 45" (7cm × 115cm) for the four-patch units and the corner blocks.

3. A rectangle 16.5" × 44" (42cm × 112cm) for the half-square triangle units.

SPECIAL NOTE ON SEAM ALLOWANCES

Imperial

Jean and I found that different circumstances call for different seam allowances. After much discussion we came up with a general rule, which is: For seams internal to the unit, block, or module you are working with, *quarter-inch seams* are most appropriate. For external seams (those around the outside edge of the block or module), which will be joined to another piece of the quilt after quilting, *half-inch seams* allow for a bit of adjustment if necessary.

To simplify the process, cut all the seams $\frac{1}{2}$", then trim the internal seams to $\frac{1}{4}$" as you go. Use the width of your presser foot to get $\frac{1}{4}$" seams where you know there will never be any adjustment—when you are joining multistrips, for instance.

Metric

When I started revising this book, I realized that I must seriously consider how to use the metric system in quilting. You can convert $\frac{1}{4}$" to 6mm when doing handwork, and that works well. But for strip piecing methods, it is not so simple. On a heavy plastic ruler, 6mm is a hard measurement to find, and 1.25cm ($\frac{1}{2}$") is next to impossible. So I have converted both these measurements as 1cm, which is a measurement between $\frac{1}{4}$" and $\frac{1}{2}$". This works very well. It makes the work much easier, and rarely do you need to trim a seam. But there is still a fraction of leeway left to you, which $\frac{1}{4}$" (6mm) seams just don't provide.

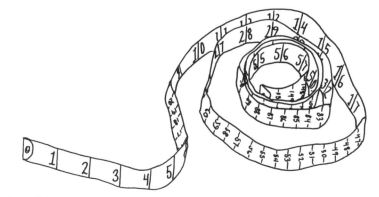

3-11. Imperial/metric tape measure.

There is probably a 1cm line marked on the sole plate of your sewing machine. It can be used to guide the edge of your fabric. To make it more visible, add a piece of tape to extend it.

Another way to get to the 1cm mark without drawing it on your fabric is to de-center the sewing machine needle as far to the left as possible. This should produce a measurement very close to 1cm from the needle to the edge of the standard presser foot. But presser feet come in many widths. My walking foot has a wide presser foot, and with the needle centered, the measurement from the needle to the edge of the foot is close to 1cm.

When you want to use your presser-foot-width as a seam allowance, measure the distance from the needle to the edge of the presser foot by putting a tape measure under the needle so that the needle comes down exactly on a centimeter mark, then lower the foot. Note the measurement to the outside edge of the presser foot. My Bernina's standard foot measures 7mm from the centered needle to the foot edge. For internal seams I double that (1.4cm) and add it to the finished measurement. I actually use 1.5cm for ease of measurement when cutting. Just be consistent when you make these decisions, and use the same measurement throughout the piece.

Also please realize that when using the metric system, I did not use literal translations of the Imperial measurements, but workable ones that produce approximately the same result. They are two different systems after all!

CUTTING THE FOUR-PATCH

1. Wash and iron your fabric to preshrink and smooth it. Accurate pieces cannot be cut from wrinkled fabric.

2. Cut the fabric using one of the following methods:

Method 1: Using the Dressmaker's Cutting Board and Scissors

This is a good method if you are not quite sure if patchwork is for you, and you don't want to spend a lot of money on special equipment. You will most probably have everything, except possibly the cutting board itself, which is not expensive and is available where you buy your sewing supplies.

Put the dressmaker's cutting board on a large, flat, firm surface. Fold the fabric so the selvages are on top of each other, and place the fabric so the folded edge is along one of the horizontal lines marked on the board. Pin in place and don't worry if the cut or torn edges along the bottom and sides don't meet perfectly. Rarely are the lengthwise and crosswise threads perfectly perpendicular.

Perhaps you will wonder why the cutting diagrams show the fabric laid out flat, but here you are told to fold the fabric. The cutting diagrams are there to suggest a way to fit all the pieces into the fabric you have bought for this project. If you study these diagrams, you will see that your work will be easier if you cut the large fabric piece into smaller sections before placing it on the cutting board. For instance, with the light fabric (Figure 3-8) you have two kinds of pieces to cut and piece. One is strips for border and four-patches. The other is squares for the triangle pieces. So if you take your 45"-wide fabric and cut it lengthwise (strips are better cut lengthwise) so that one piece contains the 16.5" rectangle and the rest is left for strips, it will be easier to handle. I would cut it at about 17.5" (45cm), which gives a bit of leeway to each piece. Then proceed with either cutting method as directed.

Place your yard/meter stick along a vertical board marking so that the first line will be drawn across a double thickness of fabric as close to the left side as possible. Move your yard/meter stick to the right the desired width, and draw another line. Continue until all the strips are marked (Figure 3-12). Pin the two layers together between the marks and cut along the lines with scissors. Cut all the strips your project requires before you start to stitch.

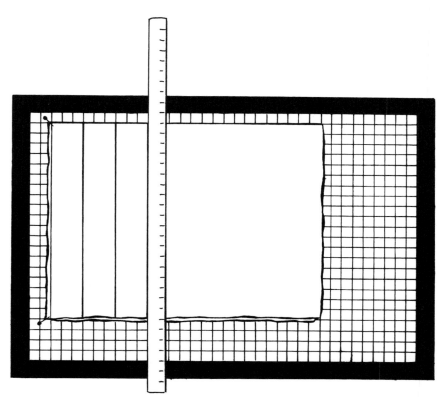

3-12. Dressmaker's cutting board.

Method 2: Using the Rotary Cutter and the Self-Healing Mat

This method is similar to the one described above, but is more accurate because you do not move the cloth while cutting. It is also quicker because you cut more layers of the fabric at one time, and no marking is needed.

Fold or stack your fabric into two to six layers and align it on the self-healing mat as for the dressmaker's cutting board. (A cardboard cutting mat *cannot* be used.) Place the fold along a horizontal line, and the uneven edges to the left side of the mat. Using a heavy plastic or metal ruler, cut as close as possible to this edge, and parallel to the vertical grid on the mat. Place your hand firmly on the ruler and run the cutter *away* from you along the ruler's edge (Figure 3-13). Then move the ruler to the

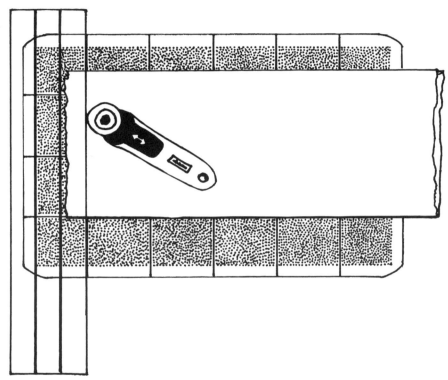

3-13. Using the rotary cutter and self-healing mat.

right for the next cut. This way, the strip you are cutting will always be protected by the ruler. (A left-handed person should reverse the process and work from right to left.) Cutting errors will not spoil the strip. If your cutter does happen to swerve or wobble, usually a narrow cut will remove the error and more strips can be cut.

Whichever way you cut your strips, if you are using folded fabrics, be sure the cut is exactly perpendicular to the fold, otherwise the strip will not be perfectly straight. Always unfold the first strip to make sure it is straight, and doesn't look like Figure 3-14!

3-14. Improperly cut strip.

STRIP PIECING THE FOUR-PATCH

1. Set up your sewing machine. The stitch length should be about 12 stitches per inch (2—2.5 on the dial). I suggest a fairly short stitch because you do not backstitch. Each strip will later be cut into segments. When one segment is joined to another, the stitches are locked in by the cross stitching. Join the long strips you have just cut, in pairs, lengthwise, a light to a dark, right sides together, using a presser-foot-width seam allowance, as this seam is one of those that will never need any changes or corrections. This makes a **multistrip.**

2. From the wrong side, press both seam allowances to one side, (usually the dark one so that the seam allowance doesn't show through the light fabric). Turn the multistrip over and press thoroughly on the front, making sure the seam is completely straight and flat. This pressing is extremely important for accuracy, and so it should be done carefully. It is not a matter of getting the fabric smooth any old way. Place the iron on the fabric and let the steam and heat do most of the work. Move the iron slowly and carefully over the surface so as not to distort the grain. Avoid large swinging motions.

3. Pin the multistrips, right side down, to the cutting board, making sure the seams are parallel with the lines on the board. Draw pencil lines across the multistrips at the required intervals (see Figure 3-15). Or lay the multistrips on the self-healing mat and using the plastic see-through ruler and rotary cutter, cut into segments.

4. Join the segments using a presser-foot-width seam. When you reverse the segments to join them, the seam allowances will lie in opposite directions, with the top seam pointing away from you (Figure 3-16).

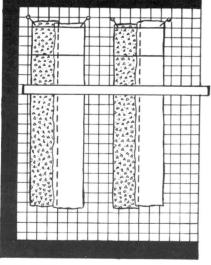

3-15. Cutting segments.

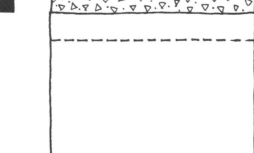

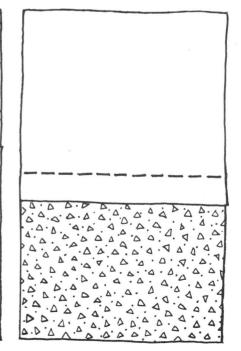

3-16. Two segments ready to be joined.

When the seams are properly aligned, you can feel with your fingers how they butt closely together (Figure 3-17). Put in a pin or two on either side of the matching seams, and stitch. After some practice, you may find the pins unnecessary if these small segments are made of 100% cotton and pressed carefully. Remember that matching the patch intersection at the cross seams is the most important thing. The ends of the rows of stitching will not show in the finished quilt, so it is not crucial that they are carefully matched. The places where the patches meet, however, must be. When you have finished all the piecing, inspect the joins. If they don't measure up to your standards, see ''Piecing the Block,'' later in this chapter, for instructions on how to correct the stitching.

5. Open the completed four-patch and press again, carefully, on both sides, keeping the seams straight and flat (Figure 3-18).

3-17. Segments butted together, ready to be stitched.

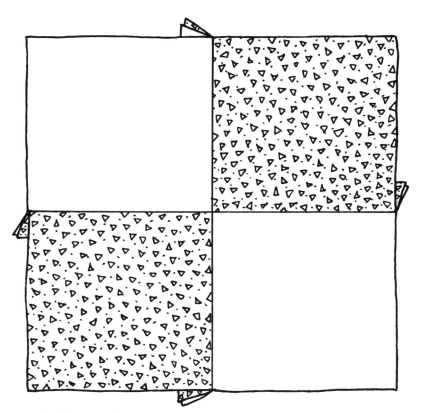

3-18. Finished four-patch.

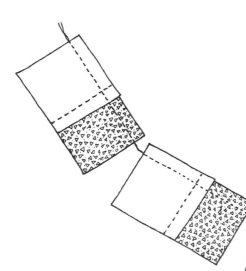

SPECIAL NOTE ABOUT ASSEMBLY-LINE METHODS

The method outlined above is most efficient when you complete one task before you begin another. That is, cut all your strips at once, then seam them all together using chain piecing, then press them all.

Chain piecing (making kite tails) means that you arrange your segments to be sewn in pairs at the side of your machine, stitch one pair together, and without breaking the thread, feed in another pair (Figure 3-19). When you have joined all the pairs, cut them apart. Press.

3-19. Kite-tail piecing.

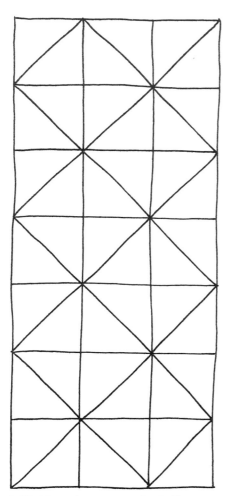

3-20. Lines drawn to make half-square triangle units.

TO MAKE HALF-SQUARE TRIANGLES WITH THE ASSEMBLY-LINE METHOD

This is pure magic, courtesy of its originator, Barbara Johannah. Though you may not recognize it as such if you have not previously pieced together any triangles, take my word for it! The half-square triangle (it has a 90° angle) is one of the most commonly used motifs in traditional patchwork. Cut and pieced singly, this unit involves a lot of work with bias seams, which are always tricky. The method Barabara Johannah has devised eliminates almost all the difficulties. It is most useful when you need a number of squares in the same color combination, but it is worth doing any time you are using half-square triangles.

The general rule when making half-square triangle units is: Draw squares 1½″ (4cm) larger than the finished dimensions of the square. This will give you two units composed of two half-square triangles sewn together with a presser-foot-width seam allowance at the bias edge where the triangles join. The "square" will not be precisely square yet. There will be ½″ (1cm) or more seam allowance around the outside edge of the squares, which you will later trim. For the Road to Expo quilt, the squares are drawn 5½″ (14cm) to give 4″ (10cm) finished units.

1. Count the number of squares in the design composed of two half-square triangles. There are 32 half-square triangle units in the Road to Expo quilt we are making (Figure 3-1).

2. On the wrong side of the light fabric, draw half the needed number of squares. Each drawn square gives two finished units, so we need 16 squares. But draw some extra squares to give yourself practice units. I drew 21. Draw diagonals from corner to corner of each square (Figure 3-20).

3. Align the two fabrics, light and dark, right sides together. Pin them together between the drawn lines.

4. Machine stitch on both sides of the diagonal drawn lines, placing the edge of the presser foot on the drawn line as a guide. Don't stitch across the intersections of the diagonals, but in a zigzag fashion around the outside of the big diamond shapes, and then along the insides of the big diamond shapes (Figure 3-21). Sometimes, depending on the number of half-square triangle units you want to produce, the stitching can all be done in one continuous line. However, it never seems to work out that way for me!

5. Cut on all drawn lines. Open the squares and press the unopened seams to the dark side of the square. Remember that these are bias seams, so treat them gently and try not to distort them. Now, in a fraction of the time taken by traditional methods, all your triangles are cut and sewn together (Figure 3-22).

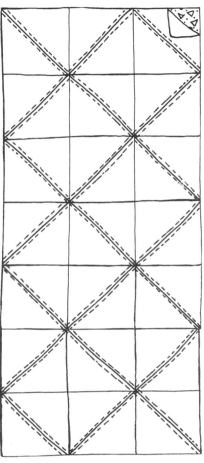

3-21. Half-square triangle unit stitching diagram.

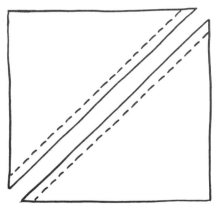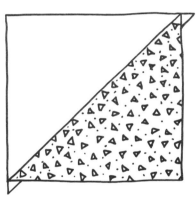

3-22. Completed half-square triangle unit.

PIECING THE BLOCK

We have now prepared a number of small units which we will join together to form the block. Each of the units is simple in itself, but each needs care and precision in its making. Beautiful patchwork is created when each piece is exactly the size it is meant to be, and each join is perfectly matched. The instructions below may seem detailed, but over the years Jean and I found that this attention to detail rewarded us with beautiful quilts.

Up to this time you have produced the elements of the block quite quickly. Now you must mark each unit with exact seam lines, for no matter how carefully prepared, these units will still vary slightly. For this purpose we make a cardboard or plastic template the size we want the finished unit to be. For the Road to Expo quilt it is 4" (10cm) square. On it mark the diagonal and the four-patch. It will be used throughout the construction of the quilt to check the size and placement of various parts of the work.

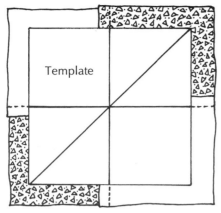

3-23. For accuracy, use a template to draw stitching lines.

Place the template on the wrong side of the pieced unit. With a pencil or pencil crayon draw the stitching line around the square template (Figure 3-23). Draw the stitching lines on all the units you have made.

Pick up the two units (a four-patch and a half-square triangle unit) and place them right sides together so that when they are joined by stitching, you will get the configuration in Figure 3-24.

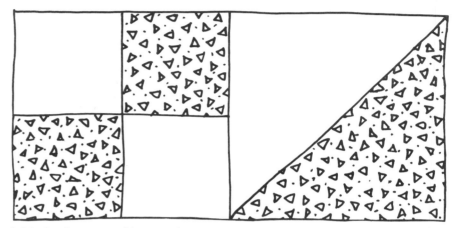

3-24. Configuration of four-patch and half-square triangle units.

Pin through the corners as shown in Figure 3-25. The pins are put along the stitching line. This method of pinning enables you to turn the piece to the right side and check that the stitching line will be in the correct place. This may not seem important at this stage in the joining process, but it will be later on. Stitch from edge to edge of the patch along the drawn line, removing pins as you come to them.

Chain piece the remaining pairs. Trim seams if necessary.

Open each pair of units and press the seam allowance to one side. In this case, press away from the triangle, toward the four-patch. As a general rule, try to keep both points of the triangle visible as long as possible in the joining process. It makes the precise joining of triangle points easier.

Now pin together two pairs of units to form the block shown in Figure 3-29. This time you will match drawn lines and intersecting seams. This matching is very important to the quality of the patchwork you will produce.

To ensure accuracy when matching triangles, take a pin and push it through the points (Figure 3-26). Hold this pin in place while you insert

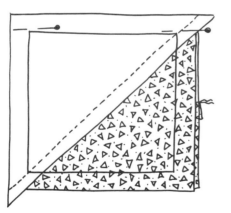

3-25. Pinning two units together.

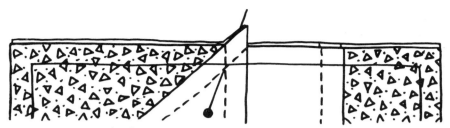

3-26. Pinning triangles for accuracy.

other pins along the seam line. Check the right side to see that the join will be exactly where you want it. Add two pins perpendicular to the seam line on either side of the join to keep it in correct alignment while stitching (Figure 3-27).

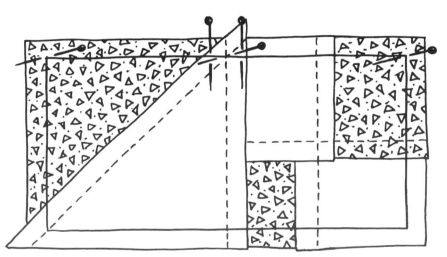

3-27. Adding perpendicular pins.

When you get to this stage, you will sometimes find that the little imperfections of the work begin to add up, and the joins do not fall perfectly into place. The most important points to match are the places where the different colored patches intersect, rather than the ends of the stitching lines. If necessary, ease any fullness between your pins. If you feel that a more perfect match is required at any join, rip open the seam about an inch (2.5cm) on either side of the error. You can do this quickly with the seam ripper (Figure 3-28). If you cut every fourth or fifth stitch, the seam will come apart easily when you pull the thread from the other side of the seam. Readjust, repin (including the perpendicularly placed pins if needed), and overstitch at each end of the repair.

Now that all the blocks have been made, the internal seams trimmed if necessary and carefully pressed, you are ready to begin

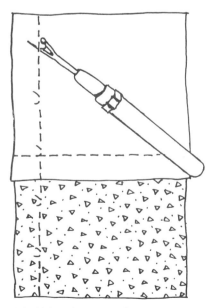

3-28. Using the seam ripper.

joining the blocks into pairs. They will be joined as shown in Figure 3-29, with one block given a quarter turn. When two of these two-block configurations are joined, the result is the module shown in Figure 3-30.

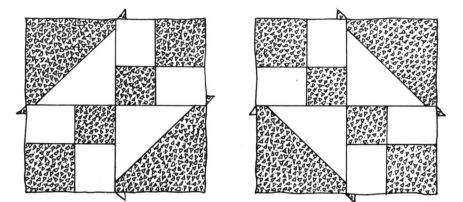

3-29. Two blocks to be joined with a quarter turn.

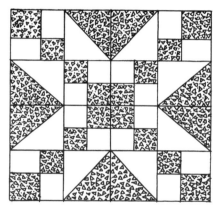

3-30. Completed module.

In the next chapter, we will layer and quilt the modules, then join them and add borders to finish the quilt.

CHAPTER FOUR

Quilting, Joining, and Finishing

TO HAND QUILT

The next section is devoted to directions for machine quilting the separate modules, but if you plan to hand quilt the entire small quilt in one piece, this is the time to join the modules with lattice strips, first in pairs with short lattice strips. The halves thus created are joined together with the long lattice (Figure 3-1).

MODULAR QUILTING UNITS

Traditionally, quilting was done on a large frame. But this is somewhat impractical for most modern houses, where all the space seems to be full of things all of the time, and there is no unused back parlor, with room for a quilting frame.

Instead, work in modular units. This does not necessarily mean block by block. Often several blocks can be worked as one module. For instance, a whole row, including short lattices, can be joined before quilting (Figure 4-1). If you use this method, the backing strip for the row

4-2. The rows of a diagonal set treated as modules.

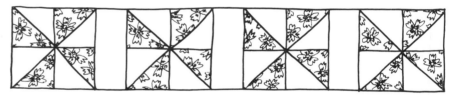

4-1. Analyze your design: any row of blocks with lattices between can be used as a module when machine quilting.

is cut in one piece the length of the squares plus their connecting lattices and the extra needed for layering. The rows of a diagonal set can be treated the same way (Figure 4-2). Sometimes the design is not composed of equal-sized blocks, but can still be broken into modules that are easy to work with (Figure 4-3).

To break a design such as that shown in Figure 4-4 into modules, consider the following:

Workable size. Twenty-five-inch (65cm) or smaller modules fit under the machine needle easily with little likelihood of uneven stitches

4-3. Unequal blocks can still be grouped (here into three rows) for quilting.

4-4. Straight set blocks.

caused by the drag of a large piece of work. But if the machine quilting you are considering changes direction a lot, it may be wise to treat each block as a module. Smaller modules are easier to turn and to work with at the sewing machine.

The hang of the finished work. This is primarily of concern when you are making a wall piece. A single central division in each direction as in Figure 4-5 hangs less well than a piece with off-center divisions as in Figure 4-6.

4-5. Central divisions to make modules.   **4-6.** Off-center divisions.

EXTENDED MODULE FOR THE ROAD TO EXPO QUILT

There are several ways to join the Road to Expo modules. We have chosen to use lattice strips and corner blocks around all sides of each module (see Figure 3-1).

1. Draw sewing lines 2" (5cm) apart, lengthwise, on the wrong side of the twelve top lattice strips. Draw lines across the ends of the strips 16" (40cm) apart. These are the lines on which you will sew when you are joining the modules together with the lattice strips. Put marks at 4" (10cm) intervals on the long drawn lines. These marks will help you make sure, when you join two modules, that the patterns will line up properly on either side of the lattice (Figure 4-7).

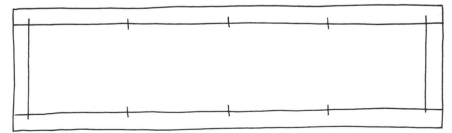

4-7. Marked lattice strip.

4-8. Extended module.

2. Draw a 2" (5cm) square on the back of the corner blocks. Sew a corner block to one end of each of six lattice strips.

3. Join a lattice strip (without corner block) to Side 1—the outside edge of the module. Press.

4. Add a lattice strip with a corner block attached to Side 2—the other outside edge of the module. Repeat with the other three modules. The modules now have lattice strips on two sides (Figure 4-8). This extended module is now ready to be quilted, then joined to the other modules.

LAYERING THE MODULES

The batting is cut large enough to underlie the extended module, half of the joining lattices (which will be added next), and the whole width of the border, which will be added last. The batting measurement is arrived at by adding together:

The extended module measurement	18" (45cm)
One half of the joining lattice	1" (2.5cm)
The width of the borders	3½" (8.5cm)
Total size of the square	22½" (56cm)

Cut the backing fabric the same size as the batting or, if possible, 1" (2.5cm) larger all the way around. The reason we cut each underlayer larger than the layer above is that matching a top and bottom layer of fabric of exactly the same size is difficult with a larger layer of batting in between. Sometimes the backing can shift in the process of machine quilting and suddenly the batting is left exposed, or there is no seam allowance left for the next step. The excess backing will be trimmed off later.

Figure 4-9 shows how the three layers of the module relate to each other, with the bottom layer being the largest of all. However, if your backing fabric did shrink a bit and your backing square is not quite as large as you would like, don't rush out and buy more fabric. Just carefully arrange the batting on the backing so that the backing completely underlies the pieced top. The excess backing fabric will be trimmed off at a later stage.

DOUBLE PINNING

Lay the batting on a flat surface. Cover it with the backing fabric, right side up. Smooth it carefully from the center, and pin the two layers together, beginning in the middle. Use safety pins for this and for the next pinning.

Turn the module over. Place the pieced top over the batting, which is now uppermost. Be sure you place it so that 3½" (8.5cm) of batting show on the two outside edges, and 1" (2.5cm) shows on the two inside edges (Figure 4-9). (These are minimum measurements—if you find you have extra batting, it can be trimmed later on.) Smooth from the center and pin through all three layers. Turn the pinned module over and remove the first set of pins. This method of pinning may seem a bit elaborate, but it almost guarantees a smooth module on which to quilt. Basting is unnecessary, and may even be a hindrance. Pinning is more flexible and can be adjusted quickly and easily if necessary.

Note that the safety pins that hold the layers together are to be inserted between the quilting lines, not on them (see Figure 4-11 for one way to quilt it).

MACHINE QUILTING

Now we are ready to begin machine quilting. It is a good idea to practice first.

1. If you have an even-feed foot, put in on the machine. This foot provides good visibility of the stitching line and helps control puckers, especially on the underside of the work, where they are the most troublesome. If you do not have an even-feed foot, a clear plastic foot or an open-toed appliqué foot is a good second choice.

2. See Chapter One for a discussion of threads. Choose a shade of thread for the machine that will blend with the fabric colors. I usually select a grayed color that will be inconspicuous in the finished quilt. I may also use a different color top and bottom. Use a fairly long stitch length.

3. Take the extra block or module you have made and pieces of batting and backing of the correct size. Layer and pin them together. Make some preliminary stitching lines on your sample. Remove it from the machine, and examine it carefully. If the machine line does not look the same on the top as it does on the bottom, try adjusting the top tension. If loops show on the top, loosen the top tension. If loops show on the bottom, tighten the top tension. When turning the tension adjustment knob, remember that "left is loose" and "right is tight." Some machines have a pressure adjustment. If you are having trouble with puckers, a lighter pressure may help.

4. Machine quilting frequently follows the seam lines to emphasize pattern shapes. This type of quilting is known as stitching-in-the-ditch. When you try it on your practice piece, you will find that, because you have pressed both seam allowances in one direction, there is a thick and a thin side to the seam. It is easier to stitch along the thin side, where there are no seam allowances. Alternatively, before layering and pinning, try pressing open the seams you plan to stitch. This makes the top as a whole smoother and flatter. I prefer this method when using slippery fabrics such as silks and satins.

4-9. Extended module pinned and ready for the quilting process.

Not every seam needs to be quilted. Synthetic batts make much larger unquilted areas feasible. Approximately 4–6" (10–15cm) can be allowed between quilting lines. The choice of where to quilt has become an aesthetic one, not a practical one.

In terms of the finished quilt design, it is sometimes desirable to stitch in places other than "the ditch." These lines can be marked on the cloth with a dotted line, using a pencil crayon in a color closely related to the thread you are using. You can use masking tape as a stitching guide for straight lines.

THE FIRST QUILTING LINE

For the first machine quilting line, choose a central one that goes right across the module, with the grain of the fabric if you can (Figure 4-10). Place straight pins along its full length, 1½" (4cm) apart, and at right angles to the stitching line. If the line begins at the edge of the module, no backstitching is required. If it must begin somewhere in the center of the block, bring the tail of the bottom thread up and take four or five stitches at zero stitch length before proceeding. Do the same thing at the end of a line if it doesn't end at the edge of the module.

Place the layered module under the presser foot where the line is to begin. Turn the hand wheel once to pull the tail of the bottom thread to the top of the work so that it doesn't become entangled in the stitches on the underlayer. Stitch slowly and carefully, using your hands to flatten and smooth the layers away from the needle. At the same time, you must remove the pins and support the work so that it does not catch on anything. Sometimes the drag caused by the sheer weight of a large piece can cause uneven stitches. Occasionally check with your fingers on the underside to see if any puckers are forming in the backing.

Whenever you stop to remove pins or adjust the work or change direction, be sure that the needle remains in the fabric to prevent any shifting of the work which would cause uneven lines or irregular stitches. When you have finished stitching the first line, inspect the back of the work to see if there are any puckers. If there is a gross error, it is better to rip out the stitches and redo them now. Sometimes you will need to redo the whole line. But if the error is minor, it may be better to wait until more quilting lines are in place. Then you can unpick between two crossing lines and remove the error (see Figure 4-12 below).

THE SECOND QUILTING LINE

When you are satisfied that the initial line looks good, put in the next line of stitching, using the techniques outlined above. Try to have this line on grain and at right angles to the first one. This tends to stabilize the piece, and any future off-grain quilting lines will be less likely to distort the shape of the module to make it off-square.

You may find that some double pinning is helpful here, especially at

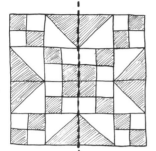

4-10. The first quilting line.

the point where the stitching lines are to cross each other. Turn the module over, top side down, and insert some safety pins so that they do not interfere with the next line of stitching, but keep the backing fabric smooth and flat. This is most helpful when the backing fabric is a polyester/cotton blend, which has little give or flexibility, and therefore must be held away from these early stitching lines to prevent tucks and puckers.

On the right side, smooth all the layers away from the place where the stitching line will go, and pin along this second stitching line with straight pins placed perpendicularly. Lower the presser foot and bring up the bobbin thread. Stitch slowly and carefully.

Continue to quilt the module, pinning, stitching and checking *each line separately*. If the stitching lines are internal to the module, bring up the under thread, lock the threads, and begin stitching from a line that you have already quilted. Stitch toward the edge of the module.

In the case of the Road to Expo quilt I have overlaid the pattern with a simple grid of quilting lines that form an unobtrusive secondary pattern (Figure 4-11). There are many ways to quilt a block, but I often use the grid. It is simple, geometric, and direct. But do give considerable thought to this additional design on your quilt. Machine lines made with a straight stitch are very strong visually.

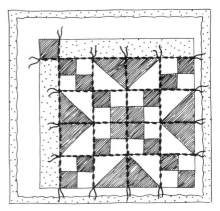

4-11. Grid quilting.

CORRECTING STITCHING ERRORS

A faulty stitching line must be removed carefully. Midway between intersecting stitching lines, clip the threads of the quilting line with the pucker in it top and bottom. Unpick stitch by stitch to the cross line of stitching (Figure 4-12). Then secure these threads as explained below. Pin the area to be restitched carefully, smoothing out wrinkles and puckers. Begin the stitching at the crossing line with both top and bottom thread tails pulled to the top so that they do not get entangled in the thread below. The tails must be long enough to secure later. Stitch to the next cross line, leaving tails long enough to sew in, as explained next.

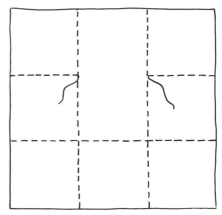

4-12. Unpicked quilting line.

SECURING THREADS THAT DO NOT GO TO THE EDGE

Draw both threads to the back of the work. Put each thread into a needle with a fairly large eye, twist the thread around the needle in the manner of a French knot, and insert the needle into the cloth as close as possible to the point where it emerged. Bring it out again after it has gone through the batting an inch or more, pop the knot through the fabric and into the batting. Clip the thread ends. If the top thread does not pull through, you can sink it the same way into the top of the quilt (Figure 4-13).

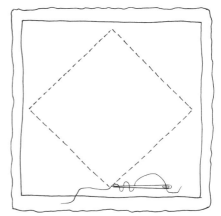

4-13. Securing threads.

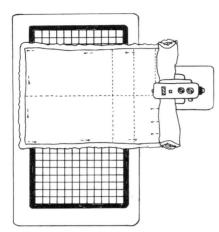

4-14. Stitching large pieces, using a table to support the work.

LARGE MODULES

You can quilt small modules wherever your sewing machine is located. When you are quilting larger modules, though, or when you are joining small ones, you must move out of your sewing corner to a larger space, where the bulk of the quilt can be supported so that the weight does not cause drag or uneven stitches. Try putting the sewing machine on a small table next to the dining room or kitchen table. This will also provide the large space needed for pinning quilted modules together. Protect the surface of your table by putting your cutting board on top of it (Figure 4-14). This figure also shows how to roll a large module to fit under the arm of the machine.

JOINING THE MODULES (QUILT-AS-YOU-GO)

The methods of joining modules are usually called quilt-as-you-go. There are a number of variations (see Chapter Five). The method you choose will depend on whether you have quilted by hand or machine, and whether your design is divided by lattice strips. The final result will be just as spectacular as those achieved by the more traditional methods. (See color section, especially The Stars are Coming Out, which is a large piece.)

For the Road to Expo quilt, the batting piece has been cut large enough to underlay the extended module, plus half of each of the joining lattices and the border. The backing fabric is a bit larger than that, if possible. The four modules have been machine quilted. Now proceed as follows:

1. Prepare the short back lattice strips. To do this, make a pressing template from thin cardboard. The template is made as wide as the finished lattice will be (in this case 2″ [5cm]) and as long as your piece of cardboard. Place it lengthwise and centered on the wrong side of the strip. Draw a stitching line down one side and on the other side fold over the seam allowance and press (see Figure 4-15.) This gives you a nice,

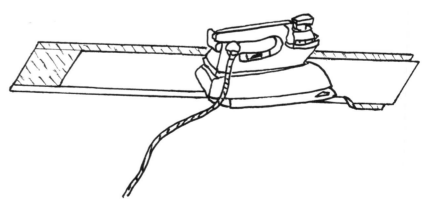

4-15. Using the pressing template.

straight, turned-under edge to hand stitch down in the final step of the joining process.

2. Layer together a short top lattice with corner block added, the quilted extended module, and a short back lattice, right sides together. Pin along the seam line, through all the layers, taking care to match the 4″ (10cm) marks on the top lattice to the unit joins of the module. Stitch through all the layers (Figure 4-16).

3. Pin, with the same careful matching, the other side of the top lattice strip to the next module. Stitch through all the layers. This joins together one row of the quilt (Figure 4-17).

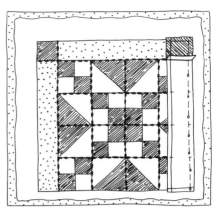

4-16. Joining lattice pinned in place.

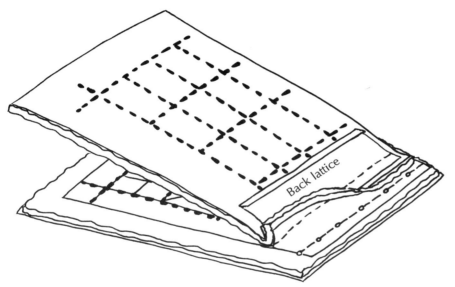

4-17. Lattice joining two modules.

4. Turn the row over, and lay flat. Check to see that the layers of batting butt closely in the middle of the lattice strip. If necessary, trim or fill in any spaces with a bit of batting whipstitched into place (Figure 4-18).

5. Fold the back lattice strip carefully over the join, covering the line of machine stitching with the pressed edge. Blind stitch into place (see

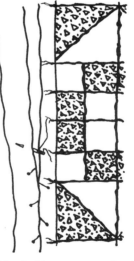

4-18. Whipstitching on extra batting to fill an area.

Figures 4-19 and 4-20). This completes the row (see Figure 4-21). Repeat steps 1 through 5 to make Row 2.

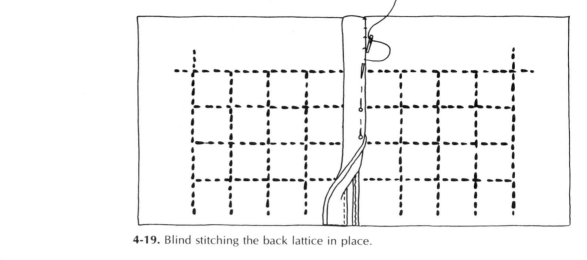

4-19. Blind stitching the back lattice in place.

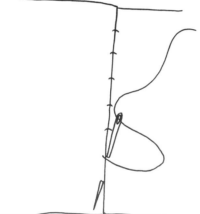

4-20. To blind stitch, take a short stitch on top, and hide the long stitch under the fabric.

4-21. One row of the Road to Expo Quilt ready to be joined to the second.

6. To join these two rows together, use the long lattice. Make the long lattice by joining a corner block, a short lattice, a corner block, a short lattice, and a corner block (Figure 4-22). Mark and press as before. Layer,

4-22. Long lattice.

pin, and stitch the long top and back lattices to the edge of Row 1 (Figure 4-23). Pin Row 2 to the other side of the long top lattice. Stitch through all the layers. Blind stitch the back lattice into place with the pressed edge just covering the machine-stitched line.

4-23. Row 1 with the long back and front lattices stitched in place, and Row 2 ready to be joined to it.

BORDERS AND FINISHING

Now that all the modules have been quilted and joined together and the body of the quilt is complete (Figure 4-24), you are ready to add the border or borders that will finish the quilt.

4-24. The two sections of the quilt are now joined. The next step is to add the double mitered border.

SEPARATE BORDERS WITH DOUBLE-MITERED CORNERS

These borders are attached to the front of the quilt with the double miter already in place, lapped over to the back, and hand sewn to the quilt.

Neat, precise borders are the ultimate finishing touch. It is surprisingly easy to achieve a beautiful frame for your quilt. The best choices for border fabrics are dark or strong colors that serve to contain the design. I usually choose colors that have been used somewhere else in the quilt. When a border is to be made of several colors, they are joined together in a multistrip and treated as a single fabric. Careful matching is needed when you are making the miter. The borders are sewn together separately from the quilt with their double miters in place. Thus they are accurately joined before being attached to the quilt and so become Never-Fail Mitered Corners!

PREPARING THE QUILT

Trim the batting to $3\frac{1}{2}''$ (8.5cm) from the finished edge of the body of the quilt on all four sides. If the batting happens not to be wide enough, whipstitch a piece of batting along the edge, and trim to the correct width.

Lay the quilt on the floor and measure each side. If you have constantly checked your measurements throughout the construction of the quilt, you should now find it to be just about as you planned it. All four sides should be equal or only slightly different in length and all the corners square. If opposing side measurements differ, choose the shorter one to use when you fit the borders, because it is simpler to ease the quilt slightly into the border than it is to stretch it out.

ADDING THE BORDERS

1. Mark the center point of each light and each dark border strip (Figure 4-25). Join one light and one dark strip together lengthwise, right sides

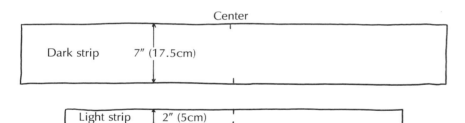

4-25. Border strips with center point marked.

facing, using the center points to match, and a presser-foot-width seam. Press the seam allowance to the dark side. Do the same with the other three sets of strips.

2. Mark lines on the wrong sides of these multistrips, measuring from their joining seam line, as follows: The line on the light strip should be 1" (2.5cm) from the seam line, and on the dark strip 6" (15cm) (Figure 4-26).

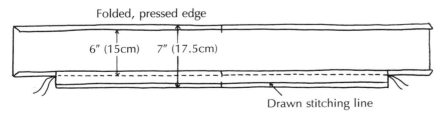

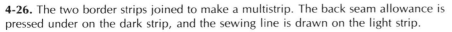

4-26. The two border strips joined to make a multistrip. The back seam allowance is pressed under on the dark strip, and the sewing line is drawn on the light strip.

Using an edge of your cardboard pressing template, turn under a seam allowance along the line marked on the dark strip.

3. From the middle point marked on each multistrip, measure outward one-half the length of the finished body of the quilt. At these two outer points, mark a perpendicular line from the stitching line to the turned-under edge of the back border (Figure 4-27). This is the baseline for the double-mitered corner. Find the center of the baseline.

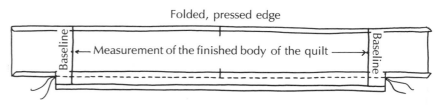

Folded, pressed edge

Baseline ←— Measurement of the finished body of the quilt —→ Baseline

4-27. The border multistrip is now marked with the baseline for the arrowhead shape (see next figure) needed to make the double mitered corner. These baselines are drawn so that the double mitered corner will exactly meet the corner of the quilt.

4. From the center of the baseline put a line at right angles, away from the body of the quilt 3½″ (8.5cm) long. Join the end of this line to the baseline on each side. This forms an arrowhead shape at each end of the border strip (Figure 4-28).

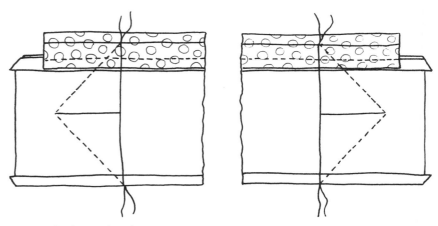

4-28. Stitched arrowheads.

4-29. The four border multistrips joined together, with the corners turned right side out.

5. Join the four strips together each to each, using the arrowhead lines, pinning carefully as they are on the bias. Check the right side to see that the strips are properly matched. Stitch, and backstitch at each end of the arrowhead (Figure 4-29). Take care not to twist a strip during joining.

6. When the four corners are joined, pin the border to the quilt, matching center markings and corners, again placing the pins along the drawn lines (Figure 4-30). Check to see that all is properly in place, and stitch

4-30. Joining the border to the quilt.

the border to the quilt from corner to corner on one side, and then to the *opposite* side from corner to corner. Finally, stitch the other two sides, carefully approaching the corners. You cannot successfully stitch around the corners. Backstitch or tie off at the end of each of these rows.

7. If everything fits well, and no adjustments need to be made, trim the arrowheads. Finger press these seams open. Turn the double mitered corners right side out over the batting. Pin and blind stitch the back border turned-under edge in place, just covering the machine stitched line with the pressed seam allowance.

8. This border is rather wide, and you may feel, as I do, that it needs a line of stitching-in-the-ditch where the light and dark strips join. Or, you may want a more complex hand- or machine-stitched design in the border. Either of these options is done *after* the final hand stitching of the border to the quilt.

BREAKING INTO THE BORDER

Breaking into the border means that the central design appears to spill over into the surrounding border and is accomplished by constructing the border of elements of the central design so that they seem to overlap into it. (See Figure 4-31 and color section for the piece Black and Yellow.)

4-31. A design that breaks into the border.

COMPLEX BORDERS

When borders are composed of pieced or appliquéd blocks, they can be treated as another module to be added to the quilt. The quilt is then bound with a narrow strip of fabric using the method just outlined for adding a wide border.

CHAPTER FIVE

More Modular Approaches

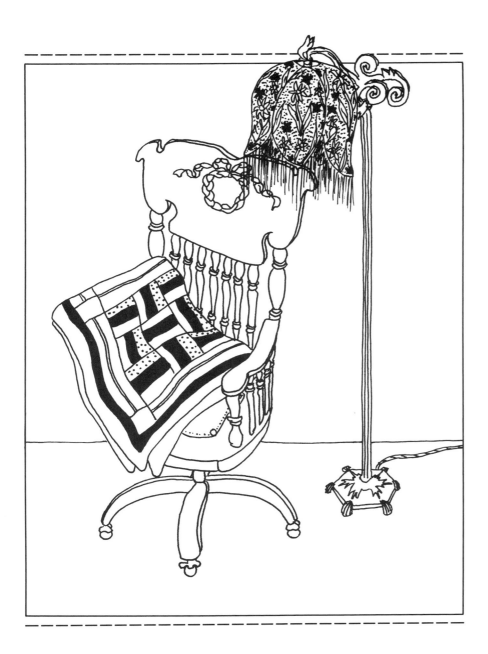

There are many ways to construct a quilt other than tackling it as one big, unwieldy unit. If you talk with other sewers about quiltmaking, they will usually speak about the complications of big frames and all that hand sewing. Well, by now you know that a big frame is not needed, and neither is hand quilting. You can design and construct the quilt in modular units that are fitted together after you quilt the three layers. In Chapters Three and Four you learned the modular system by making the Road to Expo quilt, which uses lattice strips. In this chapter we will discuss other methods that don't use lattices.

If your design does not include lattices to join the blocks or modules, it is still possible to use quilt-as-you-go methods. To use a design such as Figure 5-1, follow the directions for the Road to Expo quilt until you are ready to quilt. Take the machine quilting lines only to the outer seam lines (to where the finished edge of the module will be). Draw the threads between the backing and the batting and tie off. Then use one of the following methods:

5-1. Straight set design with no lattices.

JOINING MODULES WITH SEWN-IN BACK SEAM BINDING

This is the method I use most often in my own work.

1. Cut a strip of backing fabric the length of the seam to be joined and $1\frac{1}{2}''$ wide. Draw a stitching line $\frac{1}{2}''$ (1cm) from one long edge. Using a $\frac{3}{4}''$ (2cm) wide cardboard template, press under the seam allowance on the opposite edge of the strip. Prepare these strips for each join between two modules or two rows of modules that your project requires.

2. With small scissors, trim the batting close to the seam line from both modules.

3. Place the two quilted modules right sides together. Carefully match the intersecting joins in the two modules, and pin in place. The lines you drew earlier around the template (Figure 3-23), and which you can now see on the underside of the fabric, will help you in this aligning step. Pin the binding strip in place, using the drawn line to help with placement. Stitch through all the layers of the two modules and the binding strip.

4. Grade (trim to different widths) the seams to reduce bulk.

5. Fold the binding strip over the seams and hand stitch into place along the pressed edge. (See Figure 5-2 and the color section for large pieces made with this method, such as Black and Yellow or The Stars are Coming Out.)

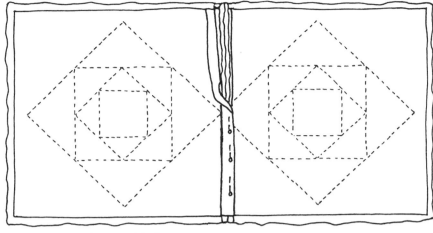

5-2. Using sewn-in seam binding.

JOINING MODULES WITH AN APPLIED BINDING

1. Trim the batting to the seam line on both modules.

2. Pin the two modules together, carefully matching the intersecting joins in the two modules. Stitch them together through all the layers. Do *not* include the seam binding. It will be added later.

3. Trim seams if necessary. Open flat with your fingers.

4. Cut a strip of backing fabric $1\frac{1}{2}''$ (4cm) wide and the same length as the stitched seam. Press a seam allowance along both edges using the $\frac{3}{4}''$ (2cm) cardboard pressing template.

5. Place the strip over the raw edges to cover them evenly. Pin and hand stitch down each side of the strip (Figure 5-3).

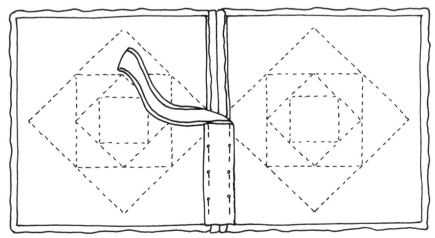

5-3. Applied seam binding.

JOINING MODULES WITH THE FLAT FELL SEAM

When you are layering the top, batting, and backing together, be sure that there will be about 1" (2.5cm) backing seam allowance along the seam you wish to finish with a flat fell seam.

1. Trim the batting to the seam line on both modules.

2. Stitch the two modules together along the seam line. Do not include a seam binding.

3. Leave one backing seam allowance intact, and grade the other three seams.

4. Fold the uncut seam allowance over the graded seams, turning under the raw edge as you go. Pin and stitch in place by hand (Figure 5-4).

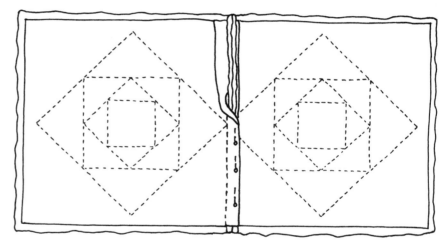

5-4. Flat fell seam for seam binding.

JOINING MODULES USING THE TRADITIONAL QUILT-AS-YOU-GO METHOD

This method is used more frequently with hand quilting because the quilting lines must stop at least 1" (2.5cm) from the seam lines of the modules. Additional quilting lines can be added across the joins after they are complete, but this is not easy to do well by machine.

1. Mark the underside of the top with the stitching lines that show you the outside edge of the modules. (These sewing lines should already be in place if you have marked each unit along the way—see Figure 3-23.)

2. Quilt all the modules. Stop the quilting lines 1" (2.5cm) from the marked seam lines where the modules will be joined to one another.

3. To join two modules, pin back the batting and backing from the marked seam line. Put the modules together, right sides facing, pin and

stitch along the seam lines, joining the top of the modules only (Figure 5-5). You can use a zipper foot to make the joining of this somewhat confined seam a bit easier.

4. Open out the two modules and place them face down on a flat surface. Trim the seams if necessary, and finger press open.

5. Trim the batting so that one piece exactly butts against the other. Flatten one backing piece out over the join.

6. Turn under the raw edge and lap the second backing over the first. (This seam should fall in the same place as the seam joining the tops together.) Pin, and blind stitch into place (Figure 5-6).

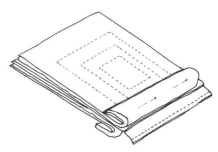

5-5. Traditional quilt-as-you-go method for joining modules, Step 1.

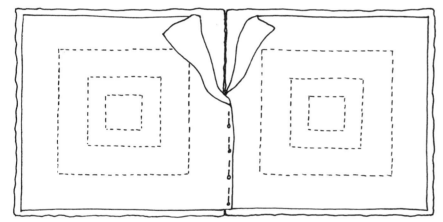

5-6. Quilt-as-you-go, Step 2.

7. Complete the rows and then join the rows together in the same way.

CHAPTER SIX

More Finishing Techniques

BORDERS MADE FROM OVERLAPPED BACKING WITH MITERED CORNERS

This technique is useful when you are making a small quilt with a one-piece backing. A similar method is occasionally used for large quilts that have been quilted on a frame.

1. Make the quilt top.

2. Cut a piece of batting the size of the finished quilt plus the width of the border you want on all four sides. Here a 2" (5cm) border is used as an example.

3. Cut the backing fabric so that it measures the size of the top, plus two border widths and a seam allowance on all four sides. Be generous. Add at least 5" (12.5cm) all the way around. Any excess fabric can be trimmed off later.

4. Quilt the layers together.

5. Turn in a seam allowance on the backing fabric and press. For a 2" (5cm) border, press under the seam allowance 4" (10cm) from where the finished edge of the quilt will be. This allows for the backing to extend 2" (5cm) from the finished edge of the quilt, and then to fold over the 2" (5cm) of batting and be stitched down on the front of the quilt.

6. At the four corners measure in from the folded edge 2" (5cm) on each side, and mark a dot A (Figure 6-1).

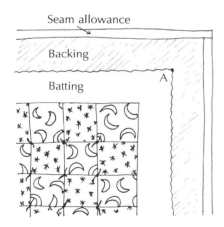

6-1. The placement of Dot A.

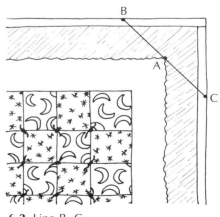

6-2. Line B–C.

7. Draw a diagonal line through this dot which will touch the folded edge at points equidistant from the corner. This makes a right-angled triangle with the 45° angles at points B and C (Figure 6-2).

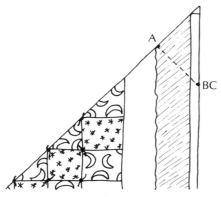

6-3. The stitching line A–BC.

8. Fold the border fabric, right sides together, so that B and C meet. Pin and stitch along the line from A to BC (Figure 6-3).

9. Trim off the extra fabric at the corners to $\frac{1}{4}''$ (1cm) from the stitched line A–BC. Finger press the seam open. Turn the corner right side out to produce the miter. Blind stitch the folded edge in place on the front of the quilt (Figure 6-4).

6-4. Front edge hand stitching.

BINDING

Binding is often used to finish the raw edges of the quilt. Although it is very narrow, it still must be considered as a design element. It can be the crowning touch or the last straw! Stripes and polka dots can make an exciting binding. (See the color section for the work Traffic Jam? in which the binding is very prominent. Compare it to Nerida Mandl's In Memorium, in which the binding is a much quieter feature of the design.)

Straight binding. Treat the narrow strips just as you would a wider double mitered border (see page 68, steps 5 to 7).

Bias binding. This binding can be used on any quilt, but is especially useful if the quilt has curved edges or rounded corners. When I use binding on a quilt, I like to make my own and apply it folded double. This is called a French fold (Figure 6-5). It is very easy to apply. Once the first row of stitching is in place, there are no raw edges left to work with. Make the binding the width you require (see below), fold it in half lengthwise, and press carefully. Then pin and machine stitch it to the front of the quilt. Trim batting and backing. Fold the binding to the back of the quilt and blind stitch in place, just covering the machine stitching line.

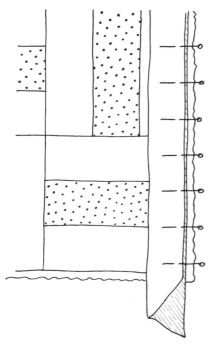

6-5. French fold bias edging.

MEASURING TO MAKE YOUR OWN CONTINUOUS BIAS

This method will produce enough bias to bind the quilt in one continuous strip. If you are going to make your own binding and apply it double as recommended, use the following table:

Imperial

For a $\frac{1}{4}''$ finished binding cut strips 2"
For a $\frac{1}{2}''$ finished binding cut strips 3"

For a $\frac{3}{4}''$ finished binding cut strips 4"
For a 1" finished binding cut strips 5"

Metric

For a 1cm finished binding cut strips 6cm
For a 2cm finished binding cut strips 10cm
For a 3cm finished binding cut strips 14cm

That is, multiply the width you wish to see on the front of your quilt by four, and add 1" (2cm) for two seam allowances. For example, $\frac{1}{2}'' \times 4 + 1'' = 3''$ (1cm $\times$ 4 + 2 = 6cm).

To determine the amount of fabric needed to produce your bias, first measure the distance around the four sides of the quilt. For example, a 90" $\times$ 90" (225cm $\times$ 225cm) quilt requires 360" (900cm) of bias. If you want $\frac{1}{2}''$ (1cm) showing, the bias strip will be cut 3" (6cm) wide. Multiply the length by the width of the bias strip required, 360" $\times$ 3" (900 $\times$ 6cm) to find the area of fabric needed. In this instance it is 1080 square inches (5400 square centimeters).

Next, determine the size of the square needed to produce this area. You can figure out the square root on your pocket calculator, or take a few educated guesses. You will find that a 33" (74cm) square seems exactly what you need. (33" $\times$ 33" = 1,089" (74cm $\times$ 74cm = 5476cm).) But there are two seam allowances needed in construction, and when marking the strips there will almost always be a small amount left that is too narrow to be usable and must be trimmed off. Therefore use a 35–36" (76–80cm) square. A square of fabric from 45" (115cm), washed, and with the selvages removed, should produce approximately:

Imperial

900" of 2" bias for $\frac{1}{4}''$ finished binding
600" of 3" bias for $\frac{1}{2}''$ finished binding
420" of 4" bias for $\frac{3}{4}''$ finished binding
360" of 5" bias for a 1" finished binding

Metric

2,000cm of 6cm bias for 1cm finished binding
1,200cm of 10cm bias for 2cm finished binding
   850cm of 14cm bias for 3cm finished binding

If your quilt is very large, or the binding wide, you may need to join continuous strips from several squares to make enough bias.

HOW TO MAKE YOUR OWN BIAS STRIP

1. Cut a square of fabric slightly larger in area than the amount of bias required. Be generous.

2. Cut the square in half along the diagonal (Figure 6-6).

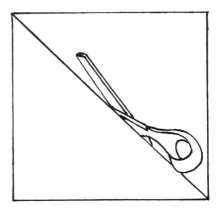

6-6. Cutting the square diagonally.

3. Join opposite straight edges, using a short stitch (Figure 6-7). Press the seam open (Figure 6-8).

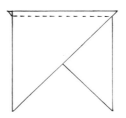

6-7. The "big-tooth" shape formed when opposite straight edges join.

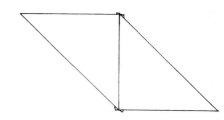

6-8. The parallelogram thus formed.

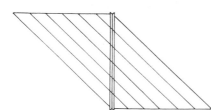

6-9. Strips marked parallel to the bias edge.

4. On the wrong side of the fabric, mark strips parallel to the bias edge (Figure 6-9). Cut off any leftover fabric not wide enough for a strip.

5. Bring together the two straight edges of the parallelogram thus formed. This makes a tube. Make the drawn lines meet, but offset one strip. Pin right sides together, matching the drawn lines $\frac{1}{4}$" (1cm) from the edge, so that the lines appear continuous. Stitch. Press the seam open.

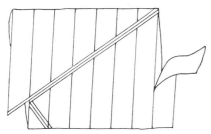

6-10. The tube being cut into strips.

6. Cut along the lines you have drawn, beginning at one of the overlaps (Figure 6-10). Now you have a unique bias tape that you can use to complete and make special any project in which it is used.

MAKING THE PARALLELOGRAM FROM A RECTANGLE

If you don't have enough fabric to make the size of square you need, you can use a rectangle of fabric that contains the same number of square inches or centimeters. The continuous bias you make will have more seams than if it were made from a square.

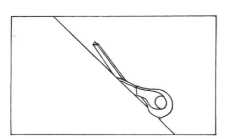

6-11. Cutting the rectangle.

Put the rectangle on the cutting board, lining up the edges with the straight lines. Draw and cut a true diagonal near the center of the piece (Figure 6-11). Stitch together the two short straight ends. Mark the diagonal lines the width you want your bias to be. Join the long straight edges and proceed as above (Figures 6-12, 6-13).

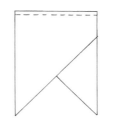

6-12. The "big-tooth" made from a rectangle.

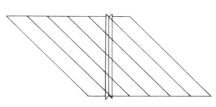

6-13. Strips marked parallel to the bias edge.

PART III
OTHER CONTEMPORARY TECHNIQUES

CHAPTER SEVEN

The Versatile Multistrip

You may not realize how much you have learned by mastering the little four-patch. The principles underlying its construction can be applied to many other patterns. You can use multistrips in several ways.

NARROW SEGMENTS

For many designs a multistrip is cut into segments the same width as the original strips (Figure 7-1). The regular repetition of a sequence of colored squares creates such designs as Sunshine and Shadow, (Figure 7-3) Trip around the World (Figure 7-2), and others (Figure 7-4).

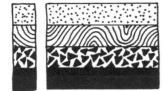

7-1. A multistrip and a segment.

7-2. Trip around the World.

7-3. Sunshine and Shadow.

7-4. Another design that can be made from multistrips.

In some designs the blocks are composed of more than one kind of multistrip. Figure 7-5 shows a nine-patch block that uses two kinds of strips.

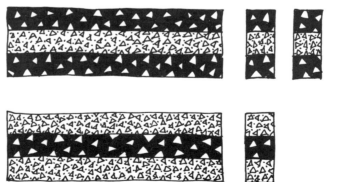

7-5. Nine-patch blocks require two different multistrips.

SQUARE SEGMENTS OF MULTISTRIPS

Another way to use a multistrip is to cut it into squares. If its width is 9" (22cm) unfinished, cut it into 9" (22cm) segments. The segments can be arranged to form many patterns (see Figures 7-6, 7-7).

7-6. Rail Fence set.

7-7. Another way to set square segments.

TRIANGULAR SEGMENTS OF MULTISTRIPS

Large or small triangles can be cut from a multistrip and used in many ways (Figures 7-8, 7-9).

7-8. Large triangles from multistrips.

7-9. Small triangles from multistrips.

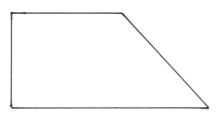

7-10. Trapezoid shape.

OTHER SHAPES

Other shapes, such as diamonds, parallelograms, or trapezoids (Figure 7-10) can be cut from a multistrip and add interest to more complex quilt blocks. Figure 7-11 and the work Rainforest I in the color section show how trapezoids and triangles can be combined in a block.

7-11. Small triangles and trapezoids cut from a multistrip make an interesting block.

HALF-SQUARE TRIANGLE UNITS

Using a multistrip as part of a quick pieced half-square triangle produces interesting results. Using plain fabric, draw a row of squares 1½″ (4cm) wider than the desired finished unit, and make a multistrip the same width. The diagonal line to guide stitching them together must always go in the same direction to produce more versatile units. (See Figures 7-12 and 7-13.)

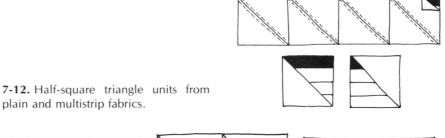

7-12. Half-square triangle units from plain and multistrip fabrics.

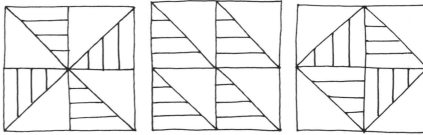

7-13. Some arrangements of plain and multistrip fabrics.

HALF-RECTANGLE TRIANGLES

When rectangles are divided in half, a long skinny triangle that is very fussy to piece is produced. Again, the multistrip comes to the rescue.

1. Make a template the size of the finished rectangle you wish to use. Draw the lengthwise diagonal on the template.

2. Cut strips the width of the rectangle plus seam allowances, and join lengthwise. Press seam carefully to one side.

3. Place the template on the reverse side of the multistrip, with the lengthwise diagonal along the seam, and draw around it with a soft pencil (Figure 7-14) to give the sewing line that you will use when you join this unit to other units in your design.

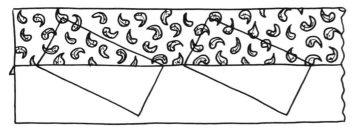

7-14. Strips can be used to make half-rectangle triangle units.

4. Move the template 1″ (2cm) along the seam line and draw around it again. Repeat until you have enough units.

5. Cut the units apart a seam allowance width from the drawn line.

6. Be careful when working with these units. The outside edges on all four sides are bias and can easily stretch. (See View to the West in the color section for an example of their use.)

COMBINING MULTIPLE PIECED UNITS

Practice analyzing quilt blocks. You will find many patterns with complex shapes which can be broken down into units you have already learned to make with quick piecing methods. You will soon see that enough block designs can be created to keep you busy for years without ever repeating a design (Figures 7-15 through 7-19).

7-15.

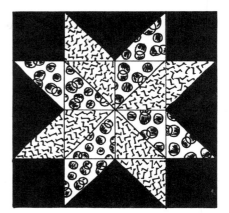

7-16.

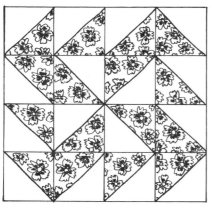

7-17.

7-18.

7-19.

SEMINOLE PATCHWORK

This patchwork technique of the Seminole Indians of Florida is probably the forerunner of modern strip pieced patchwork. The two characteristics that distinguish work of the Seminoles from other patchwork are the small scale of the work and the use of only solid colors.

Long strips are joined together as in strip piecing to form colorful bands or multistrips. The distinctive patterns of the Seminoles are made when these bands are cut into segments, often at an angle, and rejoined, sometimes by reversing or offsetting segments. One-quarter inch (.5cm) seams are used when working in this small scale. (It will be necessary to de-center the needle to get an accurate .5cm seam allowance.)

Follow these steps to experiment with Seminole patchwork:

1. Cut two strips from each of three solid color fabrics of different values. Cut these strips across the full width of the fabric. Cut the darkest strips 1¼" (3cm) wide. Cut the medium and light strips 2" (5cm) wide.

2. Stitch the three strips together lengthwise, with the narrower dark strip in the middle, to get two multistrips.

3. Press the seam allowances of one multistrip toward the light strip, and the seam allowances of the other strip toward the medium.

4. Cut each band in half. This will give you four multistrips to work with.

5. Take two of the multistrips, ones with seams pointing in opposite directions, and cut them into straight segments (Figure 7-20). These segments can be any width, but for your first experiment cut them the same width as your *unfinished* center strip (1¼″ [3cm]) so that when joined, the center strip will be square. Try a variety of arrangements and stitch them together using chain piecing (see Figures 7-21 through 7-24).

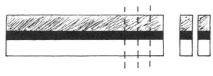

7-20. A Seminole multistrip.

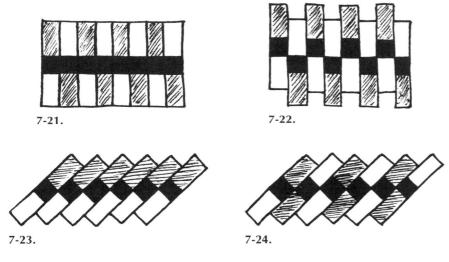

7-21.

7-22.

7-23.

7-24.

Place segments with seam allowances going in opposite directions next to each other for easier piecing.

6. Cut another multistrip at an angle. Any angle is workable. The examples illustrated are cut at a 45° angle (Figure 7-25). Draw the first line on the wrong side of your multistrip with a see-through ruler. Next, measure 1¼″ (3cm) from the line you have just drawn. Do not measure along the edge of the strip, but parallel to the drawn line. Cut, and again experiment with arrangements (Figures 7-26, 7-27).

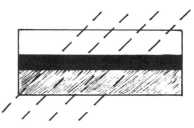

7-25. Seminole multistrip cut at an angle.

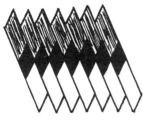

7-26.

7-27.

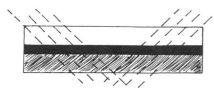

7-28. Seminole multistrip cutting lines at double angles.

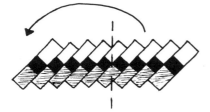

7-31. Cut the band perpendicular to the pattern.

7-32. Trim off the points.

7-33. Finish Seminole patchwork with an edging strip.

7-34. Lone Star.

7. Fold a multistrip in half cross-wise. Draw angled lines on the folded strip (Figure 7-28), then cut through two layers for the double angle chevron arrangements (Figures 7-29, 7-30).

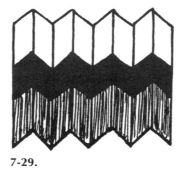

7-29.

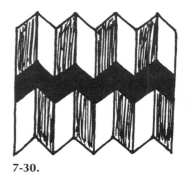

7-30.

Many pattern bands will have slanted ends. By making the ends straight, you can increase the usable length of your band. To do this, cut the band perpendicular to the pattern (Figure 7-31). Join the slanted ends. Be sure to check that the two ends will join up without disturbing the pattern. You may have to add another segment to make it work out well.

The uneven edges of many pattern bands must be trimmed. Pin the band to the cutting board so that the central pattern is parallel to one of the horizontal lines. Use two pieces of cardboard to cover the uneven edges when deciding where you would like the edging strips to be. Draw your trimming lines parallel to the central line. A see-through ruler is helpful here. Trim off the points (Figure 7-32). The completed pattern is stabilized with edging strips (Figure 7-33).

If you are thinking of using this technique in a full-sized quilt, consider the one drawback. When these designs are enlarged and offset, you must cut off large points of fabric to make the band usable. Accordingly, more fabric will be wasted than in other types of patchwork.

LONE STAR, STRIP-PIECED METHOD

Lone Star quilts can be spectacular. If made by traditional methods, a Lone Star quilt is an advanced project. Recently, however, several people have given thought to streamlining the piecing of the top. Again, Barbara Johannah's method, modified by Jean, is the one I have found most useful. It is still a more advanced project than most other strip-pieced designs you will encounter (Figure 7-34).

Careful handling of the fabric is required. Many of the seams are cut on the bias and must be stitched and pressed gently so that the diamonds are not stretched out of shape.

The Lone Star has eight identical points or arms. Each is made up of small diamonds arranged in concentric rings of color. To take advantage of the cutting board, Jean wanted to devise a method that would allow you to cut all the strips in whole inches or centimeters so that accuracy is more easily attainable. She found that a 2" (5cm) strip makes a diamond of a very useful size. The method outlined below can be used with strips of any width. Wider strips will give larger diamonds. The following formula allows you to juggle the size and number of diamonds to produce any Lone Star you want.

Use $\frac{1}{4}$" (.5cm) seam allowances if the diamonds are small—that is, if they have been made from strips up to 2" (5cm) wide. Adjust the needle position on your machine if necessary so that you can use a presser-foot-width as a guide. Use an open-toed foot so you can see where the stitches are actually going.

PLANNING THE SIZE OF THE LONE STAR

There is a ratio of 1:4.8 between the finished width of one star arm (AB) and the finished tip-to-tip measurement (CD) (Figure 7-35).

LONE STAR MEASUREMENT FORMULA

The finished width of the original strip × the number of rows in AB × 4.8 = tip-to-tip measurement (CD).

Imperial Example

If you are assembling 2" strips (finished width 1$\frac{1}{2}$") in two rows, the arm AB will measure 3". Multiply by 4.8. The finished star will measure 14.4".

AB (2 × 1$\frac{1}{2}$") × 4.8 = 14.4" (CD)

If you use four rows of 3" strips (2$\frac{1}{2}$" finished), the width of the star will be 48".

AB (4 × 2$\frac{1}{2}$") × 4.8 = 48" (CD)

You can also calculate in the opposite direction. If you want a 60" star, divide that figure by 4.8. This gives you 12.5" as the width of one arm. It could be made of eight rows of diamonds from 2" strips (8 × 1$\frac{1}{2}$" = 12") or five rows of diamonds from 3" strips (5 × 2$\frac{1}{2}$" = 12$\frac{1}{2}$").

CD ÷ 4.8 = AB

The larger the star or the more diamonds, the rougher this estimate will be.

Metric Example

We can use the same formulas as in the Imperial example to arrive at the metric measurements:

AB (finished width of rows × number of rows) × 4.8 = CD (finished width of star)

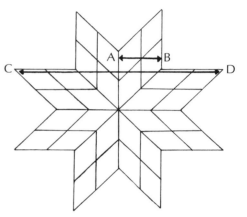

7-35. Star arm (AB) and tip-to-tip (CD).

Thus if we cut 5cm strips (4cm finished width) and use two rows in AB, the star will measure approximately 38.4cm across.

To calculate arm width from star size, reverse the process:

CD ÷ 4.8 = AB

PLANNING THE COLORS

Begin by planning one arm of the star. (This is only a color placement diagram and need not be mathematically accurate or to scale.)

1. Draw a right angle (90°) and bisect it. The acute (45°) angles formed are at the center of the star (Figure 7-36).

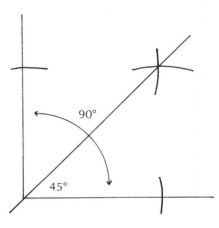

7-36. Draw a 90° angle and bisect it.

2. Add lines parallel to the bisecting line until all the diamonds in your design are formed (Figure 7-37).

3. Label the rows, and color them with crayons or with tiny fabric diamonds glued in place (Figure 7-38).

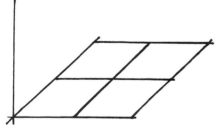

7-37. Add parallel lines to complete the diamonds.

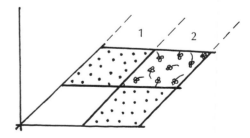

7-38. Color the diamonds.

MAKING THE STAR

I have included two slightly different techniques for piecing the star, because it is a difficult maneuver and requires precision, patience, and deft fingers. I confess my success with Method 1 was not spectacular.

Jean used it to great effect, but I found Method 2 gave me better results. So choose the one you like better.

Method 1

1. Cut one strip of fabric for each diamond in the arm you have planned. The length of the strip you cut depends on the size of the individual diamonds, not the size of the star. The strip must be long enough to cut into eight diamonds, one for each arm of the star. To find the correct length for the strip, multiply the width of the strip by 13, and then add 1" (3cm) for any measurement up to 3" (7.5cm), and 2" (5cm) for anything wider. (This should actually allow you to cut nine diamonds—one extra in case of disaster.)

Imperial

Cut 2" strips 27" long (2 × 13 + 1 = 27)
Cut 3" strips 40" long (3 × 13 + 1 = 40)
Cut 4" strips 54" long (4 × 13 + 2 = 54)

Metric

Cut 5cm strips 68cm long (5 × 13 + 3 = 68)
Cut 7cm strips 94cm long (7 × 13 + 3 = 94)
Cut 10cm strips 135cm long (10 × 13 + 5 = 135)

2. Sew one group of strips for each row in your plan. The example has two multistrips, each composed of two strips. Use ¼" (.5cm) seam allowances. Stagger the strips according to your plan to facilitate angle cutting. The amount of offset is equal to the finished width of the strips. A 2" (5cm) strip will be 1½" (4cm) wide when finished, so the offset should be 1½" (4cm). A 3" (3cm) strip will be offset 2½" (7cm) (Figure 7-39).

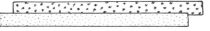

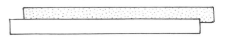

7-39. Offset strips.

3. Press all seams away from the center of the star.

4. Place the multistrips wrong side up on the dressmaker's cutting board, with one edge against a diagonal line. Pin this edge. Check the other edge to see that it is also parallel to the diagonal. If not, gently pull it into line before pinning. With the straight lines of the cutting board as a guide, use a see-through ruler and pencil to mark lines on the multistrip with the same width as your original strips. In this example the lines will be 2" (5cm) apart (Figure 7-40). For accuracy here, use the same measuring device as for the original strips.

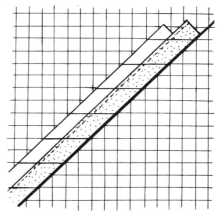

7-40. Marking for cutting segments.

5. Cut on the lines to create segments (composed in this example of two diamonds each).

6. Join together one segment of each multistrip following your plan. Stitch edge to edge using a ¼" (.5cm) seam allowance. Remember that the seams must match *at the stitching line* rather than at the edge of the segment (Figure 7-41). Press the seams toward the center.

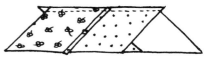

7-41. Sewing two segments together edge to edge.

7. Join the two arm units together, starting and stopping each seam $\frac{1}{4}''$ (.5cm) from the edge of the fabric. Backstitch at each end of the seam (Figure 7-42). For accuracy, in this step, you can make a template the size

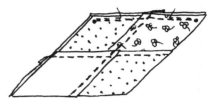

7-42. Sewing two star arms together with backstitching.

of a finished arm unit. Mark a dot with a sharp pencil on each corner of the arm units, and use these as guides when joining two together.

8. Continue to add units until the star is complete. Fan the seam allowances as you press—that is, press all the seams in one direction (Figure 7-43).

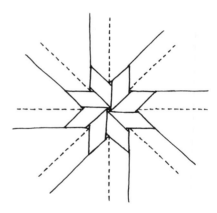

7-43. Fanning the seam allowances.

Method 2

1. Join two arm units together as above through Step 7. This makes a quarter star. Join together the rest of the units into quarter stars (Figure 7-44).

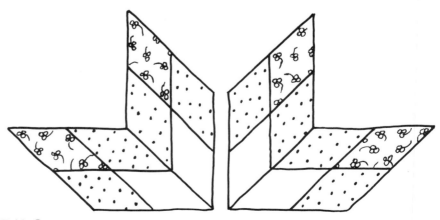

7-44. Quarter stars.

2. Join two of these quarter stars together to make half stars. Press all the seams in one direction (Figure 7-45).

7-45. Half stars.

3. Finally, join the two half stars together to make the complete star.

If, when you are using either method, the star doesn't lie perfectly flat, you can sometimes correct the situation by carefully making the seam allowances that join the arms a fraction larger. Doing so will usually eliminate any unevenness that may have been the result of slight stretching during stitching or pressing.

ADDING THE BACKGROUND

Again I have outlined two methods. I have found that Method 2, using two separate seams, works better for me, but use what suits you.

Method 1

1. Measure the length of each side of the right angles formed by the points of the arms. Using the longest measurement plus 1" (2.5cm), cut six squares.

2. Cut two of the squares in half, diagonally. Now you have eight pieces of backing fabric. Using the method outlined below, insert the squares

7-46. The completed star with background inserts laid out to produce a square.

and triangles alternately between the arms of the star so that together the background and the pieced star form a square (Figure 7-46).

3. Mark a dot on the inner corner of the right side of the insert (background) piece where the two seam allowances intersect when the backing fabric is joined to the star.

4. With right sides together, position the insert under the intersection of the star arms so that the dot is just visible when the seam that joins the two star arms is finger-pressed open. Pin the dot and this opened seam together (Figure 7-47).

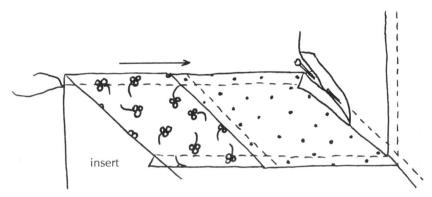

insert

7-47. Sewing in the backing insert, Method 1.

5. Using an open-toed presser foot, stitch from the point of the star to the pin. Stop with the needle in the dot on the insert. Remove the pin.

6. Raise the presser foot and pivot the work, pulling the insert from underneath and matching it to the edge of the other star arm. Lower the presser foot and continue stitching over the finger-pressed seam allowance to the tip of the star. This method requires only one seam, but is pretty tricky. It requires patience and practice.

Method 2

I have found that this method, which uses two separate seams, is easier and produces consistently good results. To begin, follow Steps 1 through 3 of Method 1.

1. Align the edge of the star with the edge of the insert. Pin it so that the end of the seam joining two arms of the star matches the dot (Figure 7-48.) Stitch to the pin, backstitching at both ends.

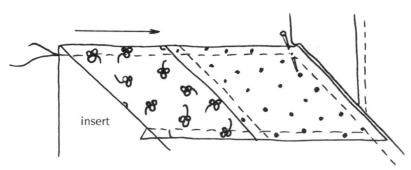

7-48. Sewing in the backing insert, Method 2.

2. Remove the work from the machine and turn it over so that the insert is on top. Align it with the other edge of the star arm.

3. Pin and stitch from the outside edge to meet, but not touch, the end of the first stitching line. Backstitch (Figure 7-49).

4. Press the seam allowances toward the star. Trim the block so that it is square and has the required seam allowances included on each side (Figure 7-50).

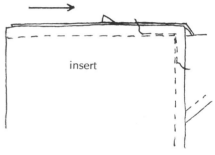

7-49. Step 3 of Method 2, with backstitching.

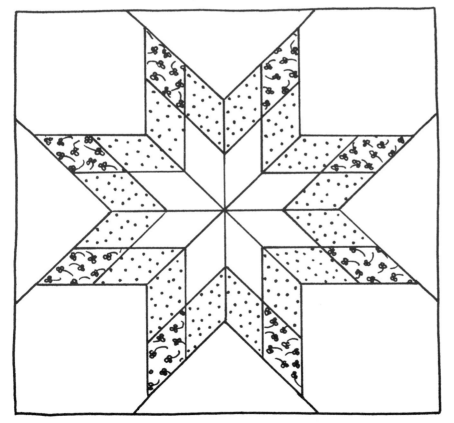

7-50. The finished star block.

CHAPTER EIGHT

Log Cabin and Strings

THE LOG CABIN

The Log Cabin is a block with a formal arrangement of lights and darks. The strips are stitched around a central square which is often said to represent the hearth and is frequently red. The strips are like logs making up the walls of the house. The color division is diagonal. Half of the square is light, and the other half is dark. This contrast makes it possible to use the blocks in a variety of configurations or sets. You are really designing with squares made up of light and dark half-square triangles.

The size of the central squares is usually the same as the width of the logs (Figure 8-1), but can be larger (Figure 8-2). The color of the central

8-1. Traditional log cabin block.

8-2. Log cabin block with larger central square.

block is consistent throughout the quilt (usually, that is, but don't be afraid to try something different). The width of the finished logs can vary from $\frac{1}{4}''$ (.5cm), as sometimes seen in old quilts, to an oversize 2″ (5cm). But they normally range from $\frac{3}{4}''$ to $1\frac{1}{2}''$ (2cm to 4cm).

The seam allowance is $\frac{1}{4}''$ (1cm), or a presser-foot-width, except on the outside set of logs. Here an extra $\frac{1}{2}''$ (1cm) is added to allow for human error. The more seams in the block, the more likely you are to need a bit of leeway.

Assembly Line Method of Making Log Cabin Blocks

This is a method devised by Barbara Johannah. It is excellent for new fabrics, or if you wish to produce a number of identical blocks. Begin by making four blocks. This will acquaint you with the method and allow you to decide whether you have made satisfactory choices in color and placement.

1. Cut a strip of fabric the width of your central square plus seam allowances, and long enough to mark four central squares plus seam allowances on the wrong side (Strip 1).

2. Cut enough strips for the rest of the logs in the width you have chosen plus seam allowances (Figure 8-3). You don't need to measure the length

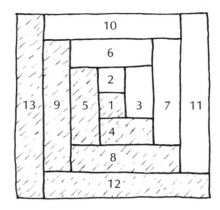

8-3. Joining sequence.

of these strips, just get yourself a pile of light strips and a pile of dark strips. Make sure the strips designated for the outside sets of logs on each block are cut $\frac{1}{2}''$ (1cm) wider than the rest.

3. With right sides together, join Strips 1 and 2 (Figure 8-4). Do not open. Cut through both fabrics on the lines marked on Strip 1. Now open and press the seams away from the central square, which is Strip 1 (Figure 8-5).

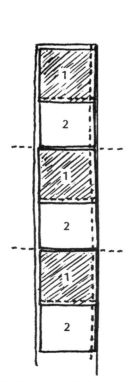

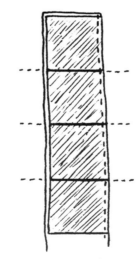

8-4. Joining Strips 1 and 2.

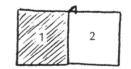

8-5. Strips 1 and 2 pressed open.

4. On Strip 3 place one of the units just pieced right side down, with Strip 1-2 on top. Stitch. Place the next 1-2 unit on Strip 3, just touching, but not overlapping, the previous unit. Continue stitching and adding new units until all are joined (Figure 8-6).

8-6. Strip 3 being added.

5. Cut Strip 3 between units to separate them. Open the new units and press the seam away from the center (Figure 8-7).

6. Add Strips 4 and 5 in the same way (Figures 8-8, 8-9, and 8-10).

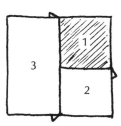

8-7. Strips 1, 2, and 3 joined, opened, and pressed.

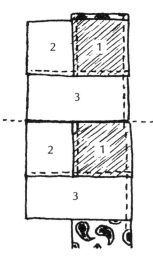

8-8. Adding Strip 4.

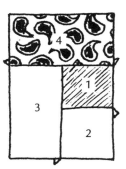

8-9. Strips 1 through 4 pieced.

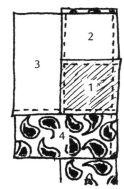

8-10. Adding Strip 5.

7. Continue adding strips, alternating two light and two dark until all pieces are joined. Always proceed in the same direction around the center.

Some Special Notes about Log Cabin Assembly-Line Techniques

This quick technique is wonderful if you go about it the right way. If you do it wrong, it's all wrong! Check the placement of the first unit each time you begin stitching a new strip. The important thing is to get the colors in the right place. When adding Strip 5 and all successive strips, make sure the stitching line crosses two seams on the correct side of the block, light or dark.

When using this method, it is not essential that all your blocks be the same. You can make any number of variations in your strips, as long as you make sure that the light strips are kept on the light side of the block, and the dark strips on the dark side.

Checking the Blocks

Lay out the four blocks in a pleasing arrangement. Stand back and view them through half-closed eyes. Is the light/dark division clear? Does one strip jump out at you? A wrong placement may go unnoticed if you are planning many different blocks, but will be highly visible if your quilt is composed of identical blocks. If you decide the blocks you have just made are not quite what you want, correction is very tedious, so don't attempt to fix them. Save them for a cushion cover or potholders, and begin again. If they are just what you want, carry on!

Cut a strip, or strips, of the center fabric long enough to mark squares for the entire project. Cut all the rest of the strips, making those for the outside logs $\frac{1}{2}$″ (1cm) wider than the others. Using this assembly-line method, make all the blocks for your quilt. Make several extra blocks. It is much easier to make extra blocks now than later.

Squaring Up the Blocks

Because of the many seams in a log cabin block, it is likely that not all the blocks will be the correct size when finished. Allowance has been made in the outer strips of each block so that you can make adjustments. Put several blocks right side down on the cutting board and measure them to see if there is sufficient seam allowance on all four sides. Sometimes there is plenty of seam allowance but the outer four logs are much wider than the inner ones. Measure across the block exclusive of these outer logs. If this measurement is more than $\frac{1}{4}$″ (.5cm) smaller than it was intended to be, reduce the overall size of the blocks you are working with.

Use the lines on your cutting board to help keep the outline square. Draw stitching lines that make all the blocks the same size, with the width of the outer logs roughly the same all around the block, even though it will not necessarily be identical block to block.

Now your blocks are ready to be laid out in various arrangements. This is an excellent way to design directly with the fabrics, bypassing the crayon and paper stage.

Log Cabin Variations

These assembly line methods of making log cabin blocks can be adapted to make variations such as Courthouse Steps (Figure 8-11), in which the logs are added not around the central square, but symmetrically, on either side. Another variation (Figure 8-12) is an off-center log

8-11. Courthouse Steps.

8-12. Off-center log cabin.

cabin block in which one set of logs (in this case the light ones) is narrower. This gives a curved effect when the blocks are joined to one another (Figure 8-13).

8-13. Off-center log cabin blocks joined together to give a curved effect.

THE USE OF FOUNDATION BLOCKS

Strings

"Strings" once referred to the long narrow strips left from other quilting projects and were traditionally used to make log cabin quilts and their variations. We still use these kinds of pieces today, but often they are cut from new fabric and placed in a more irregular way. A great variety of fabrics—all sorts of scraps and leftovers—can be used for strings. String patchwork is usually stitched onto a foundation block as it is being made. One reason for this is to create a lightweight coverlet with no filling. Another is to provide a firm base for the blocks, particularly if you are using off-grain scraps.

Choose a foundation fabric of plain, lightweight cotton, preferably white. It doesn't have to be new; old, well-washed, pressed sheets will do. Cut to the size of the finished block plus seam allowances.

8-14. Placing the first string.

Method for Covering the Foundation Block

1. Place your first string diagonally on the fabric foundation, right side up (Figure 8-14).

2. Place the second string on top of the first, wrong side up, matching the edge of the first string. Make sure that each string is long enough to cover the foundation edge to edge when folded back.

3. Stitch along the edge of the two fabrics, using the presser foot as guide (Figure 8-15).

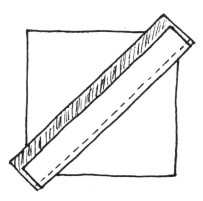

8-15. Placement of the second string.

4. Open the second piece and press flat (Figure 8-16).

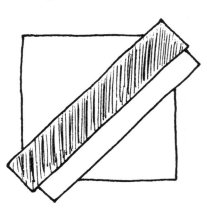

8-16. First and second strings open and pressed flat.

5. Add strings until they reach the edge of the block (Figure 8-17).

8-17. Additional strings cover half the foundation block.

6. Turn the block around, and cover the other side in the same way.

7. Press the block.

8. Trim the strings around the edges to match the foundation block (Figure 8-18).

8-18. Trimming the edges.

Variations

Strings allow for a great deal of creativity (Figures 8-19, 8-20, 8-21). Try adding them at different angles. Vary their widths. Make a her-

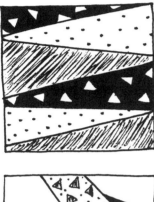

8-19. Irregular string placements.

8-20. Herringbone.

8-21. Irregular log cabin.

ringbone pattern by starting with a triangle at one edge and then adding strings alternately to both sides.

If you start with a square in the middle, you can make a log cabin. If you put the strings around it irregularly, you can get some interesting results. Take care to cover the raw end of the preceding string, and trim off any excess underneath from the previous string.

These string blocks can also be made with batting and backing as described in the next chapter.

Joining

If you have made your blocks on a foundation, you can use them as any other quilt blocks in the construction of your finished quilt.

If you have used a one-step method (see Chapter Nine), I suggest joining them by using an applied seam binding as described in Chapter Five.

One-Step Quilting and Prestuffed Units

Up to now we have been considering methods in which the quilt is a sandwich with three separate layers—top, filling, and lining, which is held together with stitches added after the layering. But there are other ways to create quilted modules. Sometimes the stitching and layering are done in one step, sometimes the middle stuffing layer is added after the top and bottom layers are joined together. These methods are explained here and in Chapter Eleven on Trapunto and Italian corded quilting techniques.

ONE-STEP QUILTING

One-step quilting is a method in which you create patchwork and quilt it to the batting and backing all at the same time. The patterns most often used are made with strings, such as Log Cabin and its variations. The same methods are used as for string quilting (see Chapter Eight), but the strips are stitched onto a piece of batting and the backing fabric instead of a foundation fabric.

You may find that when batting is included in making the string modules, the module becomes misshapen. To compensate for this distortion, we begin with batting and backing about 2" (5cm) larger than the intended finished size. There is also a certain amount of shrinkage just from the quilting.

Here's how one-step quilting works:

1. Cut squares of batting and backing fabric 2" (5cm) larger than the dimensions of the finished block.

2. Put the batting on top of the backing and lay your first fabric string right side up on the batting (Figure 9-1). Be sure it covers both layers.

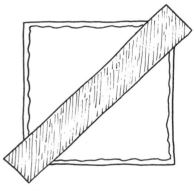

9-1. Make sure the first strip covers both layers.

3. Put the second piece on top of the first, wrong side up, matching one edge. Stitch through all the layers (Figure 9-2).

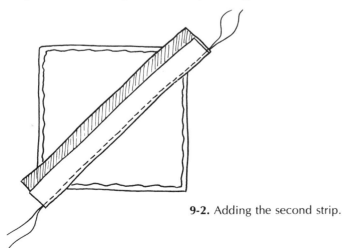

9-2. Adding the second strip.

4. Open the second piece and continue adding strips. Be sure to iron the strips well before adding them to the block, as they cannot be pressed after quilting.

5. When you have finished the machine stitching, place the module on the cutting board and mark the finished dimensions of the module plus seam allowances. Trim if necessary. Join by adding an applied binding to cover the raw edges as described in Chapter Five.

CHOOSING THE BACKING FABRIC

If the pattern you are making has stitching lines going all the way across the module (like diagonal strings in Figure 8-18), you can use a plain or patterned fabric. There are some patterns, however, such as the Log Cabin, in which the quilting lines form a rather irregular, untidy pattern on the back. For these patterns it is best to choose a small, allover, nondirectional print to conceal irregularities if you do not plan to take the extra step of lining and tying the finished quilt.

PRESTUFFED UNITS—BISCUITS OR PUFFS

Many people dismiss these puffy little units as uninteresting because many of the designs in which they have traditionally been used are rather prosaic. But when you are considering the design of your quilt, remember that each puff reads as a square. These puff-squares can be arranged to form triangles or four-patches or any of the patterns composed of these units (Figure 9-3). I have used them to show the wonderful

9-3. Prestuffed units called biscuits or puffs.

textural contrasts of velvet and silk (see Evergreen Playground in the color section).

TO MAKE PUFFS

1. Cut fabrics into squares. Almost any fabric can be used for the tops of the units, from velours and other stretchy fabrics to satins, velvets, brocades, and cottons. Usually the finished piece is completely lined;

therefore any nonstretchy fabric can be used for the bottom square. It need not even be new fabric—old sheets are fine. The top square is cut larger than the bottom square, usually by about $1\frac{1}{2}''$ (4cm). For example a finished 3" (8cm) puff is made from a 5" (14cm) top square and a $3\frac{1}{2}''$ (10cm) bottom square.

2. The top square is pinned on three sides to the bottom square, wrong sides together. The fullness is eased in by taking one or two tucks on each side. One tuck per side (Figure 9-4) gives a rounded effect to the puff; two tucks per side (Figure 9-5) gives a flatter, squarer look.

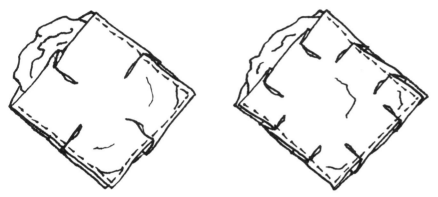

9-4. Single tuck per side.   **9-5.** Two tucks per side.

3. Stitch three sides together on the right side of the top fabric using a presser-foot-width seam allowance.

4. Fill the space between the top and bottom layers with batting scraps through the remaining unstitched side. Then pleat and stitch together the layers of the fourth side.

5. When finished, the puffs can be joined together like patchwork, first in rows, then in squares, about the size of blocks. When completed, these modules can be joined together to make the finished piece. To stitch a puff to its neighbor, put the right sides together and stitch just outside the first stitching line so that no stitching lines are visible in the finished piece (Figure 9-6).

6. Place the completed top wrong side down on a lining fabric and pin the two layers together. Tie. I prefer the ties to have their tails on the underside so that they do not interrupt the design. For making ties I use cotton crochet thread, which is strong and thick and comes in many colors. Thread a big sharp needle and push it up through the backing and the top and down again. Leave 2–4" (5–10cm) tails. Tie these into a firm double knot. Do this every 6" (15cm) or so all over the quilt. Bind the edges of the quilt.

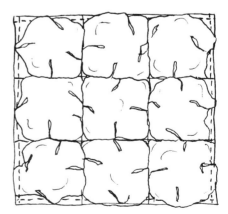

9-6. Finished puff units.

TO MAKE "SAUSAGES"

This method allows less flexibility in design, but speeds up the puff process because you make four puffs at once in the same fabric. When you see them, you will understand why they got the name "sausages."

TO MAKE A FOUR-SAUSAGE PUFF

9-7. Folded and pressed sausage unit.

1. Cut the bottom fabric $8\frac{1}{2}'' \times 4\frac{1}{2}''$ (22cm × 12cm). This will give a completed unit that measures $8'' \times 4''$ (20cm × 10cm) when finished. The top is cut $12\frac{1}{2}'' \times 4\frac{1}{2}''$ (32cm × 12cm).

2. Fold both pieces in half crosswise and press. Fold crosswise again, leaving out the seam allowance this time. Press (Figure 9-7). This marks the stitching lines.

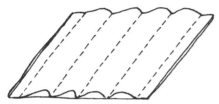

9-8. Stitched sausage unit.

3. Unfold each piece and pin the pieces wrong sides together on the fold lines. Stitch along these lines (Figure 9-8).

4. Pin little pleats between each line of stitching on one end of the unit. Stitch across the pleats.

5. Stuff from the other end with scrap batting (Figure 9-9).

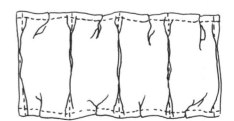

9-9. Stitch across the pleats and stuff with scrap batting.

6. Pleat the unstitched end and stitch closed. Now you have a rectangle of four puffs (Figure 9-10).

9-10. Finished sausage unit.

TO MAKE A FULL SQUARE SAUSAGE PUFF

With this method you can make even more puffs at one time. The finished unit contains eight little sausage puffs.

1. Cut the bottom fabric into an $8\frac{1}{2}''$ (22cm) square, and the top fabric into a rectangle $12\frac{1}{2}'' \times 8\frac{1}{2}''$ (32cm × 22cm).

2. Fold the bottom square into quarters and press. Fold it in half again and press so that eight rectangles are formed by the pressing lines when the square is unfolded.

3. Fold the top rectangle in half lengthwise and press. Fold again to get quarters, leaving out the seam allowance as in Figure 9-7. When it is unfolded, this piece also has eight rectangles pressed into it.

4. Pin and stitch the top rectangle onto the bottom square, matching the raw edges and pressed folds on the long sides of the rectangles.

5. Pin little pleats between the stitching lines along the center fold of the top rectangle and stitch the center line. Now stuff the puffs from both ends (Figure 9-11). Pleat and stitch up the ends.

6. Join these sausage units together in the same way as the puff squares, above.

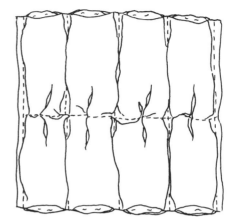

9-11. Unfinished double unit.

CHAPTER TEN

Appliqué

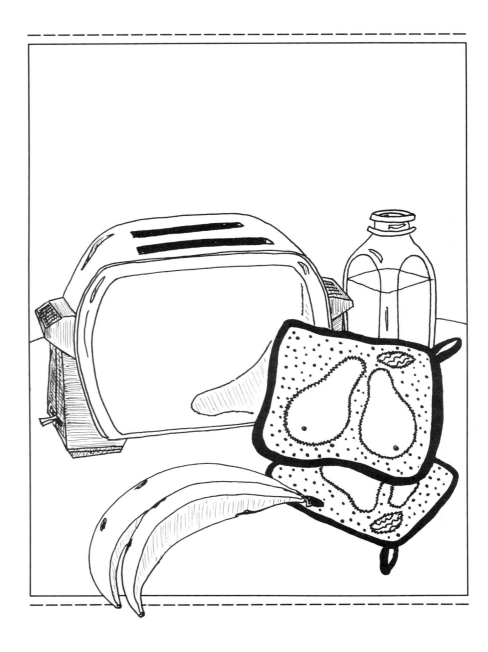

The machine appliqué method described here is by far the best I have used. People try to solve the problems of getting a nice smooth appliqué in several ways. Often some sort of stiffening is applied to the appliqué fabric before it is stitched down. I don't like this approach. Stiffening the fabric ruins the "hand" or pliability of the piece. It may be fine for an apron bib, but not for a whole quilt. In the instructions outlined below, the method itself keeps the fabric still and perfectly in place while you stitch.

Appliqué allows you to use more realistic and natural shapes than pieced work, which is geometric and abstract. Basically, the technique involves cutting a shape out of one fabric and stitching it down on another. The best of appliqué does not get bogged down in a lot of detail, but rather gives you the sense of instant recognition. It is a technique that encompasses an enormous range of possibilities. You can embark on a formal, symmetrical rendition of flowers and vines such as the Tree of Life, or you can look around your own house and garden to find shapes that can be put together to make a very personal quilt. Ice skates and lollipops, toads and daisies are fun to stitch for a child who loves them.

If you look in the color section of this book, you will find examples of the unique quality that can be achieved with appliqué. The works Cinderella by Jeannie Kamins and Baby Blanket by Wendy Lewington Coulter express charming aspects of child-centered domesticity. The messages are evoked instantly by the shapes and colors the artists have used.

To begin, choose a shape you want to incorporate into your quilt, such as an apple or mushroom. Then draw a simple outline of it. If this approach inhibits you, try cutting the shape out of scrap paper directly, without drawing it first. Just say to yourself "apple," and cut. Get the essence of the thing. You will be surprised at how successful you are. Cut a dozen apples and pick the ones you like best for your quilt.

If you are having trouble choosing a shape, look through magazines, coloring books, your Idea File (see page 11), children's books, or your postcard collection to find one that pleases you. If the shape you choose is not exactly the size you want for your appliqué, you can easily enlarge or reduce it by the following method.

TO CHANGE THE SIZE OF YOUR DESIGN

1. Place a sheet of tracing paper over the image you have selected and trace the shape.

2. Draw a square box around the tracing.

3. Cut out the box containing the drawing and carefully fold it into 16 squares (Figure 10-1).

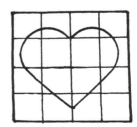

10-1. Design with 16-square grid.

4. Take another piece of paper (tracing paper is good because it is thin and folds crisply) the size you want your finished design to be, and fold it into 16 squares also.

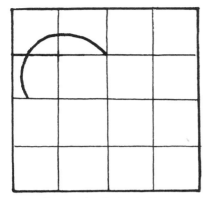

10-2. Enlarging the design in Figure 10-1.

5. Unfold both pieces of paper, and then, using a ruler and a fine colored marker, draw along the fold lines you have just made to form a grid.

6. Place the papers side by side, and carefully copy the lines from the tracing onto the new paper, square by square (Figure 10-2).

To facilitate accurate copying, note where the lines of the drawing cross the grid; mark and join these spots. For intricate sections of the design, you may need to further subdivide particular squares of both grids.

If your original drawing would fit more easily into a rectangle, use this shape instead of a square, but make the rectangle in some simple proportion such as 1:2 or 1:3 as the enlargement must be proportionately the same. For example, a drawing in a rectangle 2″ × 4″ (5cm × 10cm) can be easily enlarged to 4″ × 8″ (10cm × 20cm) or 5″ × 10″ (15cm × 30cm) but one in a rectangle $2\frac{1}{2}$″ × $3\frac{5}{8}$″ (4.9cm × 10.2cm) will pose unnecessary problems (Figure 10-3).

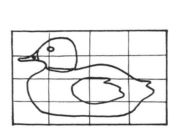
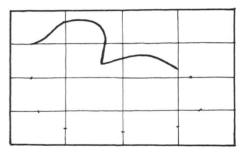

10-3. Using a rectangular format.

If the new drawing doesn't turn out exactly as you want, you can adjust it easily without redrafting the whole thing. Simply put another piece of tracing paper on top of it. Trace the lines you like from the first drawing, and change the ones you don't like. You can do this several times if you need to, until the image is just right. When you are happy with the design, make at least one copy of it so you always have the master image intact. Of course, you can follow these same procedures with any of your own thumbnail sketches or doodles.

THE JOY OF PHOTOCOPYING

For very little money, you can get copies of your drawings in sizes up to 11″ × 17″ (28cm × 43cm). Some shops can copy your drawing onto a light cardboard, which is heavy enough to serve as a one-time template when cut apart. You can also have drawings enlarged or reduced on a copier.

MACHINE APPLIQUÉ METHOD

The appliqué fabric is usually attached to the background fabric with a zigzag stitch, which is a strong visual element in itself and must be considered in the total design. Note how Jeannie Kamins deliberately emphasizes these lines by making them all black in her quilt Cinderella (see color section).

1. Using a copy of your master drawing as a template, cut out the shape.

2. From the pressed appliqué fabric, cut a square or rectangle about 1" (2.5cm) larger all the way around than the template. Place this square on top of your background fabric (also pressed) where the appliqué is to go. Put pins in the corners. It is best if the grains of these two fabrics are aligned.

3. Pin the template on top of the appliqué fabric in the correct position. Stitch carefully around its edge with a fairly short straight stitch (Figure 10-4). If you prefer, pin the uncut drawing onto the fabric and stitch directly on top of the drawn lines. When you are finished, gently tear away the paper.

4. Trim away the excess appliqué fabric as close as possible to the stitching line (Figure 10-5). A pair of sharp embroidery scissors is a boon

10-4. Position of the appliqué fabric and the template.

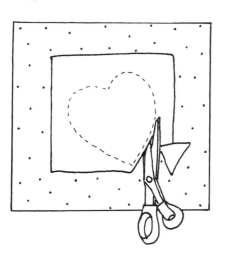

10-5. Trimming away excess appliqué fabric.

for this job. A specialized pair of appliqué scissors, with a wide flat blade on the underside, also diminishes the possibility of cutting the underfabric (see Figure 1-3). If you began with well-ironed, flat pieces of cloth, you should now have a beautifully smooth, pucker-free appliqué.

5. All that is needed to complete the design is to add a satin stitch around the outside edge. To do this you may have to adjust your sewing machine. Practice first, using the same fabrics and threads. Every machine has its own little quirks, and you must be prepared to experiment. Loosen the tension slightly. Select a short stitch, as close to ''0'' as you can get and still be moving forward, and a rather wide zigzag, usually 2.5–5.0 on the dial. When you have found a stitch you like, keep the sample and make some notes of stitch width, length, and tension, and

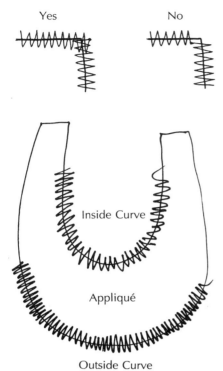

Yes   No

Inside Curve

Appliqué

Outside Curve

10-6. *Top,* Satin stitching at corners and curves. *Bottom,* Inside and outside curves.

pin them onto the sample. You can do your zigzag stitching with ordinary sewing thread. But you can get more beautiful results by using a fine sewing machine needle and special fine machine embroidery thread, which has a lovely sheen to it. Unfortunately, it is too weak to do any seam joining, and so cannot be substituted for regular sewing thread.

6. Begin stitching in the middle of a smooth line or curve, *not* at a corner, keeping the satin stitches at right angles to the edge of the appliqué. Corners and curves need special attention. To maintain this right angle, lift the presser foot frequently to adjust the angle. Always leave the needle in the fabric when you lift the foot. On convex curves, or outside corners, leave the needle in the background fabric. On concave curves, or inside corners, leave the needle in the appliqué fabric. This will ensure that the stitches overlap and do not leave gaps (Figure 10-6). Also, if you keep most of the stitch width on the appliqué fabric, there is less likelihood that the appliqué will pull away with wear and washing. A second row of stitching right on top of the first usually makes the whole thing look a great deal better. The second row of stitches should be a little bit wider than the first.

7. Bring all the threads to the back and knot them.

VARIATIONS

Sometimes you may want to add a bit of dimension to your appliqué designs, and you can easily do so with this method. If a little padding is required in one of the shapes, follow the procedure outlined above, but do not completely outline the shape with the straight stitch. Leave a small opening and add a bit of batting. Complete the straight stitching and proceed with the satin-stitched finish.

It is also possible to add filling to the appliqué by the method commonly used when filling a trapunto shape. That is, cut a slit in the backing fabric after the appliqué is finished, add some filling, and whipstitch the slit closed (see Chapter Eleven).

Machine appliqué can also be part of a quilt-as-you-go method. When you have attached your appliqué to its background fabric with straight stitching and the first row of satin stitching, layer this top fabric with batting and backing. Complete the design by doing the final row of satin stitch through all the layers.

OVERLAPPING SHAPES

Overlapping shapes are more easily straight-stitched on from the back, as follows:

1. After you have satin stitched your first appliqué shape, pin your second appliqué fabric where you want it on the right side, making sure it is flat (Figure 10-7).

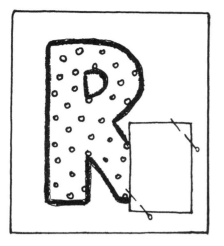

10-7. Overlapping shapes (front).

2. Turn the work to the back and position the template, using your previous stitching line as a guide to placement (Figure 10-8).

10-8. Overlapping shapes (back).

3. Straight stitch around the second template.

4. Turn the work to the front and cut away the excess fabric around the second piece of appliqué.

5. Outline the shape with satin stitch.

REPEATING SHAPES

When you wish to repeat a number of shapes in identical positions on many blocks, you can do so from the back. You can position the shapes by measuring and marking each piece or by drawing the design on the back, pinning the fabric to the front, and then straight stitching as before.

REVERSE APPLIQUÉ

This technique is one in which an underneath layer shows through holes cut in the top layer.

1. Layer the fabrics together.

2. Pin the template onto the layered fabric and stitch around it with a straight stitch.

3. Cut away the top layer with fine embroidery scissors close to the stitching line to reveal the underneath layer (see Figure 10-9). You can satin stitch for a stronger outlining of the shapes.

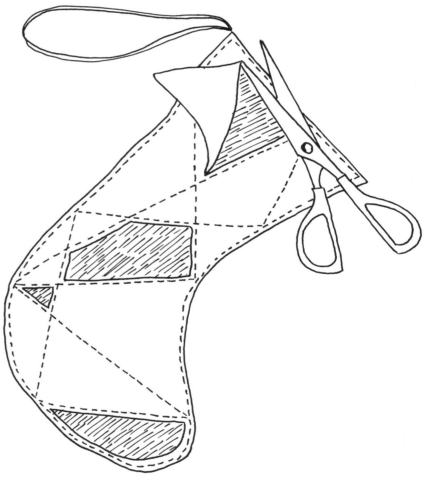

10-9. Reverse appliqué.

This technique is adapted from the Cuna Indians of Panama, who use reverse appliqué to hand stitch their colorful "molas." They often carefully piece the underlayer so that when the top layer is cut away, different fabrics are revealed in different areas. Try it!

CHAPTER ELEVEN

Trapunto and Italian Corded Quilting

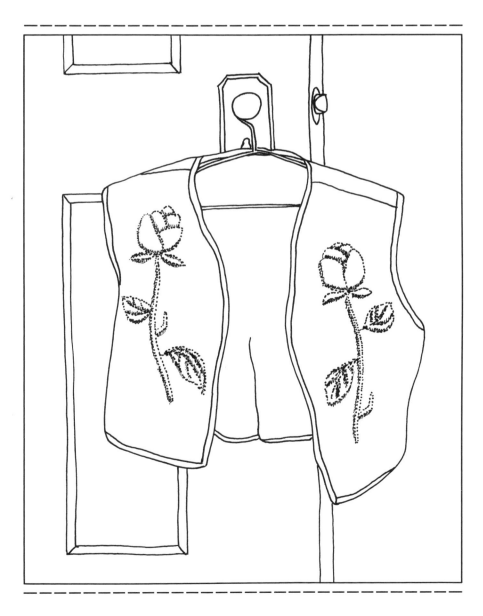

Trapunto and Italian corded quilting are elegant techniques. Rarely are they used today to make a whole quilt, but there is a very early (fourteenth century) trapunto Sicilian quilt in the Victoria and Albert Museum in London. In this quilt, figures, words, flowers, and vines are raised from the linen background by the insertion of stuffing. In a few North American museums one can also find a beautiful old whole cloth quilt, its white surface elaborately quilted, with some areas raised by trapunto to create lovely bas-relief patterns—usually flowers, wreaths, and feather patterns. Intertwined lines of Italian quilting are often used to make work inspired by Celtic design. With the aid of your sewing machine and these simple methods, your efforts will be rewarded with stunning results.

In trapunto and Italian corded quilting, the quilt sandwich is filled after the top and bottom layers have been sewn together. Any number of fabrics can be used for the top layer, but the bottom layer is usually a not too tightly woven white or unbleached cotton fabric.

Draw your design on the bottom layer. For trapunto, choose a design with enclosed spaces, such as hearts or leaves. For corded quilting enclosed spaces are not necessary because the design is created with a double set of filled stitching lines about $\frac{1}{4}$" (.5cm) apart. Traditionally, complex lines crossing under and over each other were used.

Baste the muslin backing to the top fabric, wrong sides together, and machine stitch along the drawn lines. Pull the ends of the threads to the back and knot.

TO FILL TRAPUNTO

1. Carefully cut a slit in the muslin backing within the design area.

2. With a blunt-end tapestry needle or similar instrument, insert just enough polyester stuffing to completely fill all the points and curves of the design, but not enough so that it becomes puckered (Figure 11-1).

11-1. Filling trapunto.

3. When you have stuffed all the design areas, turn the work over and check that they are not too tightly filled before whipstitching the slits closed (Figure 11-2).

TO FILL CORDED QUILTING

1. Work from the wrong side. Thread a large tapestry needle with a short length of thick wool or cotton yarn. Preshrink cotton or woolen yarns if they are to be used on clothing that will be washed later. You can use synthetic yarns, but these seem to pack down a great deal. Use as many strands as you need to fill the channel firmly.

2. Insert the needle as far along the channel as is comfortable, then bring it out, pulling your yarn up to fill the channel. Be careful with the tension here. Leave some slack when you reinsert the needle into the same hole in the channel, and proceed until the work is complete (Figure 11-3).

VARIATIONS

Double needle outline. Some interesting effects can be obtained by outlining the trapunto or corded quilting shapes with double-needle stitching. The same or different colored threads can be used in each of the two needles (see Figures 11-4 and 11-5).

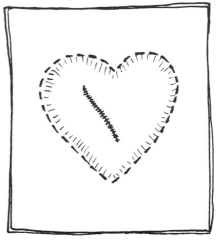

11-2. Whipstitch closing.

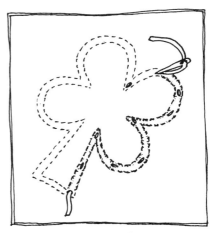

11-3. Filling corded or Italian quilting.

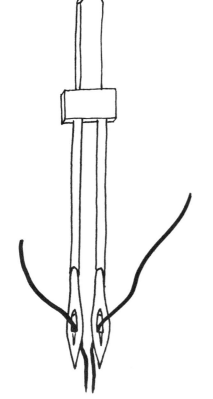

11-4. Double needle.

11-5. Trapunto design using the double needle for outlining some shapes.

Mock corded quilting. By using a double needle and tightening the bobbin tension, you get a raised effect between the needles which simulates corded quilting without the additional step of adding filling.

Colored filling. A bit of dyed fleece, or whatever other colored filling you can dream up, will add interest and give a pleasant effect under thin materials.

CHAPTER TWELVE

The Last Little Bits

CLAIMING YOUR WORK

Sign and date your work. You have just created a thing of beauty and it merits your signature on the front or on the back.

If you choose to sign your work on the front, the signature must be carefully positioned so that it becomes part of the design. You can quilt it into a block or on a border, or you can hand or machine embroider your name on the front.

You can convey more information on the piece of fabric on back of a quilt by attaching a separate piece of fabric. On it, you can embroider, type, or write the name of the quilter and the person for whom the quilt was made, the date, and the occasion. Press under a seam allowance on all four sides of the fabric square, and blind stitch it to the back of the quilt.

CARING FOR YOUR QUILT

Use your quilt, love it, and enjoy it. When it gets soiled, if it has been made of prewashed cotton fabrics and a polyester batt, wash it gently in the washing machine with a mild soap like Ivory and warm water. Tumble dry. Spread it out again on the bed. If you do not think the quilt will fit loosely into your washing machine and dryer, take it to a laundromat equipped with a large-capacity washer and dryer. Remove it from the dryer as soon as it is dry.

But don't think that because they are washable, quilts should be thrown into the machine every week. Fabrics are perishable and will eventually wear out. To prolong the life of your quilt, wash it as infrequently as possible.

For quilts made of less robust fabrics, find a good dry-cleaner. Inquire about a dry-cleaner at your local museum or art gallery. If your quilt is going to hang on a wall, be careful that it doesn't get too much light. Every few months or so, go over it with a soft baby hair brush and flick the dust off. Or, if your vacuum cleaner has one of those little round brushes, put a layer of fine netting over it, lower the suction, and vacuum your quilt.

If a quilt must be stored for any length of time, do not wrap it in plastic. Roll the quilt, top side out, in an old, well-washed sheet so that the wrinkles will be on the underside of the quilt. If the quilt cannot be rolled, but must be folded, be sure to refold it in different ways now and then. Keep it in a cool, dark, dry place.

HANGING A QUILT FOR DISPLAY

If you decide to hang your quilt, do so carefully. Each quilt should have enough space around it so that viewers can appreciate it by itself, as a beautiful object.

If you are involved in planning and hanging a quilt show, be merciless in insisting that each piece have room to breathe. Nothing is more detrimental to the good name of quilting as an art form than a huge room with rows and rows of quilts close together, sometimes overlapping or folded.

Never use nails or sharp clips through the quilt to hang it. These will damage the fabric. Tabs protruding over the top of the quilt to take the hanging dowel seldom add to the overall design. A concealed sleeve attached to the back of the quilt near the top is best.

I prefer to make the hanging sleeve from the backing fabric if there is enough. It can be pieced from scraps. If there is not enough fabric left, use washed muslin or other cotton fabric.

1. Cut a fabric strip 6" (15cm) wide and 1" (2.5cm) shorter than the width of the quilt. Turn under and stitch $\frac{1}{2}$" (1cm) double hems at each end. Press.

2. Join together the two long edges of the strip, wrong sides together, to make a tube. Press the seam open and at the same time press the tube flat so that this seam is in the middle of one side.

3. Pin and hand stitch the sleeve into place (with the seam underneath) on the back of the quilt, close to the top (Figure 12-1). When the sleeve is

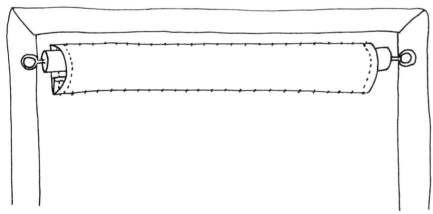

12-1. How to hang a quilt on the wall.

applied like this, the quilt itself is not touched by the wooden dowel that will be inserted into the tube to support the weight of the quilt. The dowel should be the same length as the finished sleeve, and about $\frac{3}{4}$" (2cm) in diameter. Insert a screw eye into each end of the dowel. The screw eyes should not protrude over the edge of the quilt, so that the hanging apparatus is not visible. This will give the quilt even, invisible support.

4. Put nails in the wall so that they will go through the screw eyes, or put invisible nylon fish line through the screw eyes and hang the quilt from nails near the ceiling. I use the fish line method because I often rearrange the things that are hanging on my walls, and I can use the same nails each time, regardless of the size of the piece being hung. Do not place a quilt in strong or direct light.

MAILING A QUILT

Sometimes you will need to send your finished quilt to someone living far away. This is the only time that plastic is ever used for packing a quilt, in this case to protect the quilt from any moisture that may inadvertently come its way. Fold and roll the quilt loosely in an old sheet or pillowcase, then put it in a large plastic bag and seal it up. Now find a strong cardboard box that it will fit into. Seal this up and wrap the box in strong brown paper. This is an important parcel. I send mine by registered mail so that it can be traced if lost and can be insured. I also get a return reply card so that I know it has reached its destination and that somebody has signed for it.

Be sure the recipient receives instructions from you, the maker, on how to hang, store, and clean the quilt. I have had a card printed that I include with each quilt that leaves the studio (Figure 12-2).

Quilt Name and Date

Textiles should be protected from light, dust and abrasion. Please keep this piece out of direct sunlight and clean with care. Occasional light vacuuming with a net-covered nozzle brush will remove surface dust. Bed pieces made from cotton and cotton-polyester blends may be folded loosely and machine washed and dried in warm or cool water with Ivory Soap flakes on gentle cycles. Other pieces should be dry cleaned by a reputable firm. To store, roll or fold the piece loosely, right side out, in a well washed cotton sheet. Refold occasionally. Do not use plastic for storage.

Pat Cairns

12-2. Care card.

THE NEXT AND FUTURE QUILTS

Now that you have read this book, you know the basics. You can look at a quilt or pattern and decide whether it can be made with the new, quicker machine techniques, or whether it must be done more slowly, by hand. You can gather your fabrics, all washed and pressed, make a mock-up, and work out a color plan. You can sew your design quickly and accurately and produce a lovely quilt.

Many quilts are made for commemorative reasons. They may be a loving response to life's events such as the birth of a baby, a wedding, or a new home. Once you master the techniques, you can create your own special images or continue, and perhaps reinterpret, old patterns.

Remember that anything you make says something about you and how you view the world. But don't be overawed by this—your personal statement can be very simple. Your quilt can say, "I love you," "I'm crazy about red," or "This apple shape is marvelous." Or it can convey a whole family history or celebrate an entire city.

When you are in the designing stage, give yourself time to think, to drift, to daydream—the very antithesis of how we have been told we should spend our time. That is why quilting retreats and courses of a week or more are so valuable. In two hours or two days one is too busy to think, too busy to allow the designing right brain to take over. While pressure is sometimes helpful, it often results in a solution that is only minimally good.

Keep small notebooks around you for jotting random thoughts that may come to you in the midst of a busy, rushed day.

WORKING IN SERIES

You may begin to realize that the pieces you are making have a connectedness. You are working in a series, really. Something about what you are working with—the color, the design, the message—is interesting enough to you so that you want to have another try. For instance, some of the work illustrated in this book has become part of a Star Series, which, in turn, is part of a larger theme having to do with the sky, and what one sees in it, or portrayed against it.

I feel that my work shows me standing on a middle ground, using traditional elements, but trying to do so in a contemporary way that says this quilt was made in the 1990s, not the 1890s!

The Variable Star, or Ohio Star, has been part of my work for some time. It appeals to me because it can be made from simple units, squares and half-square triangles, and can be used in so many ways. In the large piece The Stars Are Coming Out (see color section), a light center gradually darkens toward the outside edges. The stars show strongly only in the transition areas. In fact, they are not really important. The color change has become the subject.

But in the pieces Two Blue Stars and The Stars at Night … (see front cover and color section), the star shape is prominent. The traditional pattern has been disrupted, as in Two Blue Stars, where the whole star is not used, or as in The Stars at Night …, where the stars have been slightly moved from their traditional perfectly repetitive positions in the pattern grid. If I had not made several other quilts that incorporated this star, I would probably not have spent enough time ruminating about the star configuration to understand that these kinds of small innovations make for interesting work. So I urge you to continue to play, either with paper and pencil or directly with the cloth, and be willing to experiment and make mistakes. Don't hurry. Speed isn't everything.

Remember also that in making a quilt you can combine several techniques. Unique fabrics can be created by hand or machine embroidery, by printing, using linocuts, potato prints, rubber stamps, silk screens, cyanoprints, or photocopies. You can paint on fabrics or crayon them. You can tie or stitch and dye them or use wax or other resists to form patterns. The quilt Disappearing Forest by Louise Slobodan is made from individually silk-screened blocks, carefully designed and printed to express her ideas of concern about the environment (see color section). The bibliography lists interesting texts and periodicals that will tell you more about these techniques.

So you can see that really, the end of this book is just the beginning. Now that you have come this far, perhaps you can understand my passion for the medium and will join me in the lifelong pleasure of making quilts with a contemporary flavor and seeking out other quilts, old and new, to study and appreciate.

Bibliography

There are many wonderful books about quilting. Look in your local quilt supply store, browse in the library, and don't forget mail-order catalogs and secondhand stores. Here you will often find books on subjects other than quilting, that didn't sell very well the first time around, but that are full of great photographs on some odd subject like sunsets on the Florida coast or the vanishing post boxes of Britain. Perhaps they will give you a starting point for some unique project of your own, as well as a lot of visual enjoyment.

The books I have listed below are mostly concerned with visual ideas or with stimulating creativity in some way. The techniques for making quilts are, with patience, easily learned, and if you practice the things you have learned from this book, you should have the capability to make almost anything you can dream up.

BOOKS

American Quilt Study Group. *Uncoverings*. Yearly volumes of scholarly papers on the history of women's textile arts and the social context surrounding them.

Barker, V., and Bird, T. *The Fine Art of Quilting*. E. P. Dutton, 1988. This book concentrates on contemporary quilters as artists. At least one page is devoted to each artist, with a statement about her approach and a color illustration.

Beyer, J. *Patchwork Patterns*. EPM Publishers, 1979. All you need to know about drafting any pattern you want, any size.

Brackman, B. *Clues in the Calico: A Guide to Identifying and Dating Antique Quilts*. EPM Publishers, 1989. A reference for those who want to learn about old quilts.

Cooper, P., and Buferd, N.B. *The Quilters: Women and Domestic Art— An Oral History*. Doubleday Anchor Books, 1978. Interviews with pioneer women in Texas whose quilts gave meaning to their lives.

Dodson, J. *Know Your Bernina*, 2nd ed. Chilton, 1988. One of a series of books designed to increase your use and enjoyment of your particular brand of sewing machine.

Edwards, B. *Drawing on the Right Side of the Brain: A Course in Enhancing Creativity and Artistic Confidence*. J.P. Tarcher, 1979, revised 1990. The subtitle says it all. An aid to getting the courage to do your own thing.

Embroiderers' Guild Practical Study Group. *Needlework School*. Chartwell Books, 1984. A comprehensive, fully illustrated guide to all sorts of embroidery.

Ericson, L. *Fabrics ... Reconstructed: A Collection of Surface Changes.* Eric's Press, 1985. Innovative ways to manipulate fabrics that can be used in clothing or quilts.

Fanning, R., and Fanning, T. *The Complete Book of Machine Quilting.* Chilton, 1980. A veritable dictionary of hundreds of techniques.

Fassett, K. *Glorious Knitting.* Century, 1985.

———. *Glorious Needlepoint.* Century, 1987.

———. *Glorious Color.* Century, 1988. Fassett is an eminent colorist. Each book is full of vibrant, wonderful color use. Read, look, enjoy, and you will learn a lot!

Granick, E. W. *The Amish Quilt.* Good Books, 1989. Many color plates. The color choices made by the Amish women often seem modern to our eyes. This book gives much information on this special group of people.

Gutcheon, J. *A Quilter's Guide to Fabric: Probably More Than You Ever Wanted to Know about Making Cotton Prints for Quilters in the 1990's.* Gutcheon Patchworks, 1990. Interesting technical discussions of how prints are made. Poor binding.

Hargraves, H. *Heirloom Machine Quilting.* C.&T. Publishing, 1990. Revised edition of an earlier work, which shows you how to make machine quilting simulate handwork.

Hopkins, M.E. *It's Okay If You Sit on My Quilt.* ME Publications, 1989. Simplifies and categorizes designs and techniques.

Horton, R. *An Amish Adventure: A Workbook for Color in Quilts.* C.&T. Publishing, 1983. A series of exercises on the use of an Amish color palette.

———. *Calico and Beyond.* C.&T. Publishing, 1986. Discusses principles of combining printed fabrics and using unusual fabrics.

———. *Plaids and Stripes: The Use of Directional Fabrics in Quilts.* C.&T. Publishing, 1990. The latest "old-made-new" category of fabrics used with style throughout.

Johannah, B. *The Quick Quiltmaking Handbook.* Pride of the Forest Press, 1979. A truly revolutionary book that began the new, faster methods of piecing and cutting used by most quilters today.

Koroluk, B. *Your Quilting Primer.* Lormac Publications, 1988. Well-presented lessons for beginning hand quilters, written by a home economist whose daughter has a quilt shop!

Kyle, M., ed. *Quilt Digest Book 1.* Kiracoffe & Kyle, 1983.

———. *Quilt Digest Book 2.* Kiracoffe & Kyle, 1984.

———. *Quilt Digest Book 3.* Quilt Digest Press, 1985.

———. *Quilt Digest Book 4.* Quilt Digest Press, 1986.

———. *Quilt Digest Book 5*. Quilt Digest Press, 1987. Well-written articles and beautiful illustrations on many aspects of contemporary and traditional quilting.

Laury, J.R. *The Creative Woman's Getting-It-All-Together-at-Home Handbook*. Hot Fudge Press, 1985. Established artists who work at home tell how they do it.

———. *Quilts and Coverlets: A Contemporary Approach*. Van Nostrand Reinhold Company, 1970. This book really started me on my quilting career. Her approach is truly upbeat, modern, and relaxed.

Leman, B., and Martin, J. *Log Cabin Quilts*. Moon over the Mountains Publishing, 1980. Gives many methods for making this traditional favorite in a wide variety of designs.

Leon, E. *Who'd a Thought It: Improvisation in African-American Quilt-making*. San Francisco Craft and Folk Museum, 1987. An interesting look at a quilting tradition where unmeasured piecing allows great variation in the repetitions and creates its own kind of rhythms.

Leone, D. *Fine Hand Quilting*. Leone Publishing, 1986. Detailed instructions for making traditional quilts with lots about hand quilting.

Martin, N.J. *Threads of Time*. That Patchwork Place, 1990. Beautifully photographed old quilts with instructions on how to make similar ones today.

Mathews, K., ed. *The Fiberarts Design Book Three*. Lark Books, 1987. Showcases designs in all fabric media selected from thousands of entries and gives an exciting overview of contemporary work. There are two previous volumes and another on the way.

McCloskey, M., and Martin, N. *A Dozen Variables*. That Patchwork Place, 1987. The authors take a simple star pattern and show you how to color it in many ways, as well as combine it with other blocks.

Pellman, R., and Pellman, K. *The World of Amish Quilts*. Good Books, 1984. A reference book of color and design in Amish quilts, plus a description of the Amish way of life and how the designs are derived from their surroundings.

Porcella, Y. *A Colorful Book*. Porcella Publishing, 1986. Few words, many pictures of this exciting artist's work and her inspirations.

Poster, D. *Speed-Cut Quilts*. Chilton, 1989. Gives many patterns and quick cutting methods to make them.

Proctor, R., and Lew, J. *Surface Design for Fabric*. University of Washington Press, 1984. Many methods for creating a unique printed fabric from simple tools to use in your work.

The Quilt Engagement Calendar, compiled by Cyril I. Nelson, Dutton Studio Books. Each year this beautiful collection of quilt photographs, mostly of traditional pieces, gives access to unusual designs, one for each week.

Quilt National Catalogues. Every two years the Dairy Barn in Athens, Ohio, has an open competition called "Quilt National," which is for all living quilters. It has become an international showcase for contemporary work. Here are the catalogue titles:

> *The Quilt, New Directions for an American Tradition.* Schiffer, 1983.
> *Quilts: The State of an Art.* Schiffer, 1985.
> *Fiber Expressions: The Contemporary Quilt.* Schiffer, 1987.
> *New Quilts: Interpretations and Innovations.* Schiffer, 1989.

Quilting by Machine, Singer Reference Library, Cy DeCosse, 1990. Lavishly illustrated guide to sewing machine techniques.

Rush, B. and Wittman, L. *The Complete Book of Seminole Patchwork.* Madrona, 1982. Out of print, but the most comprehensive overview of this technique and its origins.

Schaefer, B. *Working in Miniature.* C.&T. Publishing, 1986. Excellent design and technique for those who like to work on tiny things.

Walker, M. *Complete Book of Quiltmaking.* Knopf, 1986. Good on design and modern techniques, with an English flavor.

PERIODICALS

I have included addresses here so you can write for up-to-date subscription rates.

The Clarion: America's Folk Art Magazine. Quarterly. Museum of American Folk Art, 61 West 62nd Street, New York, NY 10023. This beautifully produced magazine is part of the museum membership. Quilts are often included.

Fiberarts: The Magazine of Textiles. Bimonthly. Nine Press, 50 College Street, Asheville, NC 28801. Showcases new talents and innovative ideas in all textile media.

Quilter's Newsletter Magazine. Ten issues yearly. Leman Publications, Inc., 6700 West 44th Avenue, Wheatridge, CO 80033. The first and best of the quilting magazines. Very informative on shows, competitions, and other events of interest. Also includes articles on quilters, patterns, instructions.

Quilting Today. Bimonthly. Chitra Publications, Box 437, New Milford, PA 18834. One of the newer quilt magazines. It covers a mixture of traditional and contemporary work with excellent color reproduction. It also announces coming events and gives instructions for projects.

Surface Design Journal. Quarterly. The magazine is included in the membership of the Surface Design Association, Inc., 4111 Lincoln Blvd., Suite 426, Marina Del Ray, CA 90292. Professional and exciting journal that profiles contemporary artists, reviews shows, and discusses techniques. Excellent color coverage.

Threads Magazine. Bimonthly. Taunton Press Inc., 63 Main Street, Newtown, CT 06470. The kind of magazine I really like. Eclectic as to techniques, beautiful photography, lots of inspiration.

Visual Arts Newsletter. Five times yearly. Alberta Culture and Multiculturalism, Visual Arts, 3rd Floor, Beaver House, 10158 103 Street, Edmonton, Alberta, Canada, T5J 0X6. *Free.* Informative articles on all aspects of life as a visual artist from shows and portfolios to hazards in the studio.

Suppliers

There are interesting shops selling quilting supplies everywhere. Investigate the Yellow Pages and see what you can find near you.

In Vancouver, where I live, there are many places to find interesting fabrics. There are discount houses where the selection is never the same twice, and the customer must know what she is buying. You may find that the price is terrific, but the fiber content is 100% unknown!

There are also various ethnic areas where exotic and beautiful things can be found. The Punjabi market has cottons, silks, and sari fabrics with gold and silver entwined. In Japantown are handwoven ikats and in Chinatown, rich silks.

Do investigate areas of your own town or nearest city which might not be on your usual routes. You may be in for a delightful surprise when you leave the malls and high-rent districts!

If you love to get things by mail as I do, or you are interested in receiving information from quilting organizations, here are some addresses for you to try.

Aardvark Adventures, Box 2449, Livermore, CA 94550. (415)443-2687. A wonderful mail-order source for books, a huge selection of exotic threads for embroidery, and notions like you've never seen before. Also an information-packed newsletter called *Aardvark Territorial Enterprise* when you become a customer.

American Quilter's Society, P.O. Box 3290, Paducah, KY 42002-3290. Offers members discounts on books; presents annual show. Year's membership fee is $15; write for details.

Beaver Island Quilts, 155 Beaver Island, St. James, MI 49782. Gwen Marston and Joe Cunningham offer quilting workshops each autumn; they fill up early in the year. Gwen and Joe also market their own excellent videotapes on all phases of quiltmaking, and they've written some good books.

Cabin Fever Calicos, P.O.Box 550106, Atlanta, GA 30355. Quilt books, notions, fabrics, batting.

The Cloth Shop, 4415 West 10th Avenue, Vancouver, Canada V6R 2H8. (604)224-1325. A delightful shop selling fabrics, notions, books, patterns, and stenciling supplies. Quilting lessons. Mail order catalog.

Clotilde, Inc., 1909 SW First Ave., Ft. Lauderdale, FL 33315. Threads, books, videos, needles, pins, notions, Ultrasuede scraps, generic sewing machine feet. Catalog available for $1.

Come Quilt with Me, P.O. Box 021063, Brooklyn, NY 11202-0023. Pat Yamin's catalog offers quilting tools, videotapes, and books—lots of good stuff.

The Cotton Club, Box 2263, Boise, ID 83701. Unusual fabrics by mail.

Crazy Ladies and Friends, 1606 Santa Monica Blvd, Santa Monica, CA 90404. This is Mary Ellen Hopkin's store; stop in and visit. You can also order Mary Ellen's books, quilting tools, and T-shirts.

Dicmar Trading Co., P.O. Box 3533, Georgetown Station, Washington, DC 20007. Marie Carr's catalog, "The Whole Quilting Book List," is available from this address.

Dorr Mill Store, P.O. Box 88, Guild, NH 03754-0088. 100% wool in solid colors. $3 for two color charts.

Dover Street Booksellers, P.O. Box 1563, 39 E. Dover St., Easton, MD 21601. Extensive selection of books.

Exotic Silks, 252 State St., Los Altos, CA 94022. Silks. Complete set of swatches $20; if swatches returned in a month, $18 refunded.

The Fabric Carr, P.O. Box 32120, San Jose, CA 95152. (415)948-7373. Professional ironing supplies, sewing notions, books.

Fabrics in Vogue, 200 Park Ave., Suite 303 East, New York, NY 10266. Membership charge.

G Street Fabrics, 11854 Rockville Pike, Rockville, MD 20852. All fabrics mail order, custom service. $2 swatch service.

Hancock Fabrics, 3841 Hinkleville Rd., Paducah, KY 42001. (800)626-2723, orders only.

In the Beginning, 8201 Lake City Way NE, Seattle, WA 98115. (206)533-8862. Great selection of fabrics and good newsletter telling about classes and quilts to view.

Kaye Wood Publishing Co., 4949 Rala Road, West Branch, MI 48661. Videotapes and books, quilting supplies, and specialized tools, including a cutout square template.

Keepsake Quilting, P.O. Box 1459, Meredith, NH 03253. Books, notions, fabrics, lamé samples, batting.

Lacis, 2990 Adeline, Berkeley, CA 94703. New and antique laces. $1.50 for catalog.

Madeira USA Ltd., 30 Bayside Ct., Laconia, NH 03247-6068. High quality threads, yarns, and flosses.

Maiwa Handprints, #6, 1666 Johnston Street, Granville Island, Vancouver, Canada V6H 3S2. (604)669-3939. Fabric painting supplies and books by mail order. Also has a quarterly *Newsletter for the Fiber Artist,* which is free and has excellent information on dyeing techniques, books, and workshops.

Nancy's Notions, Ltd., P.O. Box 683, Beaver Dam, WI 53916. Books, videos, notions, fabrics, fusibles. Free catalog.

Newark Dressmaker Supply, Box 2448, Lehigh Valley, PA 18001. (215)837-7500. Mail-order source for almost all sewing supplies. Free catalog.

Open Chain Publishing, P.O. Box 2634, Menlo Park, CA 94026. Source for *Singer Instructions for Art Embroidery and Lace Work, The Complete Book of Machine Quilting,* and many others.

The Perfect Notion, 566 Hoyt St., Darien, CT 06820. Notions.

Quilters' Fancy Ltd., 2877 Bloor St., West Toronto, Ontario, Canada M8X 1B3. (416)232-1199. Fabrics, books, patterns, courses. Free mail-order catalog.

Quilters Helper, Box 519, Main St., Osgoode, Ontario, Canada K0A 2W0. (613)826-2501. Books, notions, fabrics, cross-stich, and smocking supplies by mail order.

Quilters' Resource, Inc., P.O. Box 148850, Chicago, IL 60614. Lamés, all types of threads and glitz supplies.

Quilting Books Unlimited, 1158 Prairie, Aurora, IL 60506. Large selection of quilt-related books. Catalog, $1.

Quilts & Other Comforts, Box 3944, 6700 W. 44th Ave., Wheatridge, CO 80034-0394. Patterns, templates, books, kits, and accessories. These are the same people who publish Quilter's Newsletter Magazine and Quiltmaker. Catalog is $2.50.

Seventh Ave. Design-Fabric Club, 701 7th Ave., Suite 900, New York, NY 10036. Membership charge.

Sew Art International, P.O. Box 550, Bountiful, UT 84010. Invisible thread, other unusual threads.

Speedstitch, 3113 Broadpoint Drive, Harbor Heights, FL 33983. Sulky metallic threads, invisible threads, Sulky rayon threads, machine embroidery supplies. Catalog $3 (refundable with purchase).

Treadleart, 25834 Narbonne Ave., Lomita, CA 90717. Decorative and utility machine threads.

Great Places to See Quilts and Textiles

Most museums in North America have some quilts tucked away in their collections, but the ones listed below have good textile collections or frequently mount shows featuring fabric arts.

American Museum of Quilts and Textiles, 766 South Second Street, San Jose, CA 95112, (408) 971-0323. Regularly changing exhibits feature quilts and textiles from around the world and the museum collection. The focus is on twentieth-century work. Housed in a charming, small, Spanish-style house and garden.

Esprit Collection of Amish Quilts, 900 Minnesota Street, San Francisco CA 94107, (415) 648-6900. Splendid private collection of Amish quilts, well displayed in the beautiful old warehouse building that is now the Esprit headquarters. A self-directed tour with catalog allows you to enjoy the quilts at your own pace.

Museum of American Folk Art, 2 Lincoln Square, New York, NY 10023. There are often quilts among the beautifully displayed objects in this gallery.

The Museum of Textiles, 55 Centre Avenue, Toronto, Canada M5E 2H5, (416) 599-5515. A large and varied collection, mostly ethnic costumes and Oriental rugs. They have the unusual and wonderful policy of allowing you to touch the exhibits on display in their many galleries.

The New England Quilt Museum, 256 Market Street, Lowell, Mass. 01852. A new museum established, appropriately, in an old New England textile manufacturing town. Changing exhibitions and a beginning collection.

The Royal Ontario Museum, Bloor Street at Avenue Road, Toronto, Canada. A world-class museum with splendid Oriental collections. For many years woven coverlets and quilts from the pioneering days in Ontario have been collected.

The Textile Museum, 2320 S Street, Washington D.C. 20008. (202) 667-0441. A collection of 10,000 textiles. Through exhibitions and publications the museum encourages appreciation for the beauty and significance of cloth.

Index

About the Author

Pat Cairns was born and has lived most of her life in the west coast city of Vancouver, Canada. Her early training was in pharmacy, which she practiced for several years in Toronto, London, England, and Southern Rhodesia, now Zimbabwe. She stopped working to raise three daughters and decided not to return to pharmacy. Instead she enrolled in a school for textile artists when she began to have time to pursue her own interests again. There she took classes in weaving, spinning and dyeing, silk screen printing, tie dye, blockprinting, and drawing, but quilts and the sewing machine won her heart, and she began making machine-sewn quilts and teaching others how to make them.

Today, she shares a spacious studio with two other textile artists on Granville Island, a part of Vancouver where many artists and craftspeople have studios. She invites you to visit her when you come to Vancouver.

She has had several one-person shows, and was part of a four-woman show called Transforming Tradition, which traveled to six galleries across Canada. She was one of six artists commissioned to make a quilt for a pavilion at the Expo '86 World's Fair in Vancouver. She has also executed many private commissions.